WAGES, PRICES, PROFITS, AND ECONOMIC POLICY

WAGES,
PRICES,
PROFITS,
AND
ECONOMIC
POLICY

Proceedings of a Conference
held by the Centre
for Industrial Relations,
University of Toronto, 1967

Edited by JOHN H. G. CRISPO

University of Toronto Press

Copyright Canada 1968
by University of Toronto Press
Reprinted 2015
ISBN 978-1-4426-3956-0 (paper)

Foreword

The Conference at which these papers were presented was planned with one purpose in mind. The decision to hold the Conference was made after it became clear that the Economic Council of Canada was going to devote a substantial portion of its *Third Annual Review* to the relationship between wages, prices, and profits and to the effects of this relationship on the trade-off between full employment and stable prices. The Centre decided that a forum should be provided where the Council's views on these subjects could be aired and scrutinized.

This objective dictated the format of the Conference. Provision was made not only for an ample statement of the Council's findings, but also for a review of those findings by a number of independent scholars and labour and management representatives. The calibre of the presentations that were made was so high that we decided to publish all of them. We are convinced that they will make a significant contribution to the literature in this field.

The Centre is grateful to all of those who participated in the Conference, as well as to those who attended, for making it such a worthwhile experience. We would also like to thank Miss Carolyn Johnson and Mrs. Elinor Smith for administering the Conference and for preparing the various manuscripts for publication. Finally, we are indebted to Mrs. H. V. Nelles of the University of Toronto Press for her editorial assistance.

JOHN H. G. CRISPO

Contents

WAGE-PRICE-PROFIT
RELATIONS IN CANADA

INTRODUCTION, by H. I. Macdonald

In the traditional language of economics this Conference covers at least two-thirds of that unholy trinity: production, distribution, and exchange. In the more recent jargon, it encompasses a large part of what we now refer to as microeconomics. In terms of social implications it touches upon the wealth of the nation, the welfare of its people, and the wisdom of its governments. Looked at from close range, the pace at which we develop the capacity to deal with economic problems seems petty indeed; yet how far we have come from that simplistic, linear concept of economic relationships that prompted David Hume to write in his *Political Discourses* (1752): "The greatness of a state, and the happiness of its subjects, however independent they may be supposed in some respects, are commonly allowed to be inseparable with regard to commerce; and as private men receive greater security, in the profession of their trade and riches, from the power of the public, so the public becomes powerful in proportion to the riches and extensive commerce of private men."

Today, in contrast, our concern is focused upon wages policy, after-tax profits, wage-price guidelines, and the right combination of monetary and fiscal policy. However, just as recognition of the complexity of economic problems and policies has grown, so our capacity to contend with the issues has expanded, in no small part as a result of the efforts of men like John Deutsch, chairman of the Economic Council of Canada.

In the same essay to which I referred earlier, David Hume paid tribute to "that rare class of thinkers" who are also advisers: "They suggest hints, at least, and start difficulties which may produce very fine discoveries when handled by men who have a more just way of thinking." Politicians who must, after all, demonstrate a "just way of thinking" have reason to be indebted to Dr. Deutsch, for the first three reviews of the Council have not only suggested hints, but also have produced very significant discoveries.

It is fitting then that we should ask the man who has become a prophet in the profession of our subject to present the first paper.

Wage-Price-Profit Relations in Canada: The Problem in Perspective

JOHN J. DEUTSCH

The Economic Council of Canada has been occupied with matters of wages, prices, profits, and economic policy both because they arise out of its general duties and because of a specific reference made by the Government of Canada in 1965. At that time the Council was asked:

(1) To study factors affecting price determination and the interrelation between movements in prices and costs and levels of productivity and incomes.

(2) To report on their relationship to sustained economic growth and to the achievement of high levels of employment and trade and rising standards of living.

(3) To review the policies and experience of other countries in this field and their relevance for Canada. (*Hansard*, March 22, 1965, 12,621)

These questions are inherent in the problem of achieving our economic and social aims. The act of Parliament which established the Economic Council in 1963 directed the Council to study and advise upon the medium- and long-term development of the Canadian economy in relation to the attainment of the basic economic and social objectives which are set forth in the act. Briefly, but more specifically, these goals are: full employment, a high rate of economic growth, reasonable stability of prices, a viable balance of payments, and an equitable distribution of rising incomes.

Of course, it is one thing to set forth desirable goals; it is quite another thing to achieve them. From the outset the Council has tried to recognize and to give warning about the inherent difficulties:

Recent history has shown that few, if any, of our economic and social goals can be expected to be realized automatically. A brief review of the operations of the Canadian economy since the Second World War . . . indicated that during this relatively short period, we have encountered at one time or another inflation, unemployment, slow rates of growth and crises in the balance of payments. This experience serves well to demonstrate that the real problem lies not in how to pursue some particular objective, but in how to achieve *all* our agreed social and economic goals simultaneously and consistently. The various goals are not always compatible with each other. Policies designed to accomplish a particular aim such as full employment or rapid rate of growth may be in conflict with the policies needed to avoid inflation or to maintain a viable balance of payments. There is always the overriding requirement to reconcile conflicting tendencies and to achieve consistency. Otherwise, the objectives are not likely to be attained either collectively or separately over the longer run (*First Annual Review*, p. 2).

These problems of conflict and reconciliation are heightened by the "rising expectations" of our times. We now speak about the problems of living with prosperity. A most apt newspaper report on the situation in the United States is also appropriate here:

It's a fact of life—and an irony too—that when an economic boom is approaching its peak or has just passed it, more people are distressed than was the case in poorer times.

High living often results in economic indigestion.

Today's economy in the United States is on nearly the highest plane in the country's history, but economists, politicians, brokers, cabinet officers, businessmen and students are carping as never before.

The complaints are endless. Prices are high, goods are shoddy, taxes burdensome, stocks declining, wages out of line, good manners and service at a new low. Nobody can agree on how to resolve the situation, least of all the politicians.

The distress is enough to make some adults wish aloud for the good old days when, they claim, they were a little bit poorer but a good deal happier.

Nevertheless, in a material way, a good argument can be made for saying this is the nearest the U.S. has ever been to being "a promised land."

When the economy nears a limit, as it now may have, relations tend to become strained. Growth slows. The same effort as before doesn't produce the same result as before.

The wage-price-profit relationship clashes instead of meshes. Out of line, the friction produces inflation. Efficiency is the victim.

Arguments break out. Economists talk of slowing the economy, of putting on the brakes through less spending or more taxes. But the problem is political as well as economic.

Businessmen complain that profits are eroding as the economic strains make their operations less efficient. And workers find their pay cheque isn't going as far as it used to go.

In looking for solutions to these problems we are likely to be confronted by a series of dilemmas. As Professor Solow, of the Massachusetts Institute of Technology, accurately described the situation: "It is precisely when economic analysis and economic policy are pretty successful, when the economy is poised near where it ought to be, that it becomes impossible to foresee with any delicacy exactly what will be required next." To examine the "problem in perspective," as I was asked to do, it is necessary to look at Canadian developments in the light of those occurring in other parts of the world, in the light of past experience, and in the light of the choices available.

The economic and social objectives which we have adopted in Canada are very similar to those of other modern industrial countries. All of these seek to achieve full employment, high rates of economic growth, etc. Also, all of them have encountered conflicts, difficulties of reconciliation, and sometimes outright failure. However, before we explore this experience in detail we should take a look at the over-all result.

On the whole the modern industrial countries have turned in a remarkably good record since the end of the Second World War. Postwar reconstruction was quickly accomplished, world trade was re-established on a far healthier basis than had existed for many decades, and real incomes per capita were doubled in less than a generation. The success attained in all these matters stands in sharp contrast to the tragic failures of the interwar period. There have been no disasters since the Second World War which could possibly compare with the hyperinflation in Germany in the early twenties nor with the general mass unemployment of the thirties. There have been lesser difficulties of course, but we can safely say that the industrial countries have learned the bitter lessons of the interwar period at least well enough to have prevented similar tragedies from happening in our own time.

For a long time the recurrence of mass unemployment was a great curse. This curse led to the postwar adoption of full employment as a prime objective of public policy, and I think it can be said now that this has been achieved with a considerable degree of success. It is true that there have been some distressing short-falls from time to time, especially in North America, and at other times and in other places there has been some tendency to have over-full employment, but these shortcomings have been a matter of degree, rather than of outright failure. With regard to prices and financial developments, things have not been ideal in the various countries. But again there has been no serious instability or general break-down.

These are some of the considerations we should keep in mind as we try to look at the problem in perspective. The progress which we have made during the last twenty years in attempting to achieve our basic economic and social goals has certainly been substantial. But, of course, it has been less than ideal, and far less than completely satisfactory. Now we are concerned about how we can overcome the remaining deficiencies and how we can accomplish further improvements. In trying to assess the nature of this task in Canada, it is useful to look at what has been happening elsewhere.

There are some quite significant contrasts between Western Europe and North America and within North America between Canada and the United States. The countries of Western Europe have generally strongly emphasized the goal of full employment. These countries have been highly sensitive to unemployment, and they have used monetary and fiscal policies very actively to keep the unemployment rates at low levels. Over the past ten years, they have generally succeeded in keeping the unemployment rate within a range of 1 to 2½ per cent of the labour force. In Western Germany, the rate has frequently been less than 1 per cent, and in Sweden it has rarely gone above 1½ per cent.

On the other hand, over the same recent ten-year period, unemployment in Canada and the United States has averaged something more than 5 per cent of the labour force and has never, in either country, fallen as low as 3 per cent on an annual basis during the past decade. These differences between the two sides of the Atlantic are quite significant. They arise partly out of a different set of priorities in public policy, but also out of important differences in circumstances. In Western Europe the growth of the labour force has been extremely small over the past decade, and in the chief industrial countries of Europe labour has been a very scarce factor of production. In Canada and the United States, on the other hand, the labour forces have been growing rapidly compared with historical standards. Moreover, in Canada our labour force has been growing at a rate at least 50 per cent greater than that in the United States and has by far the greatest rate of growth of any in the industrial world. Arthur Smith has noted recently that in the last six years total employment in Canada has increased by a figure which is as large as that which has taken place in the United Kingdom and West Germany put together over this period. Enormous contrasts of this kind inevitably have important implications for public policy and for how economic and social goals can best be achieved.

There has also been a considerable contrast between the two sides of the Atlantic with respect to the development of prices. In Canada and the United States over the past fifteen years consumer prices have risen on the average about 2 per cent a year. In the countries of Western Europe, this average has been close to 4 per cent a year. Western Germany is an exception. Over this same period, European money wages have risen on the average about twice as rapidly as they have in North America. From the middle of the fifties until a year or so ago average unit labour costs in manufacturing in Canada and the United States remained remarkably stable and over this entire period changed very little. In the countries of Western Europe, on the other hand, there have been significant and persistent increases in average unit labour costs of production. The differences in attitude and concern are well illustrated in the testimony given recently before the Special Joint Committee of the Senate and House of Commons on Consumer Credit by Professor Kragh, the Head of the National Institute of Economic Research in Sweden:

It might be useful to you to compare a country which is quite similar in many respects to Canada as far as resources go, and political stability and relative importance of exports, economic growth and so on, which nevertheless has quite a different experience in the field of price development, which I understand is the main theme for this afternoon.

Just to give the general idea about the difference, I looked up the Canadian figures for price development—consumer prices—in the years 1959 to 1965, and I found that there was an 8 per cent increase over this six-year period. This, from a Swedish point of view, is quite an amazingly stable price development. We had during the same period a 25 per cent increase that is more than 4 per cent per year on the average. If you take out the Consumer Price Index, the increases caused by indirect tax changes, we get a somewhat lower figure, but it is still from 19 to 20 per cent, which is more than double your rate of increase.

You will understand, therefore, that I was not very much impressed when I heard yesterday the Governor of your central bank complain about the price development in Canada. He said he saw no comfort in comparing prices with other countries, and I understand him to some extent because, as the United States is the largest trading partner of Canada, you, in the first place, have to look at the American price development. It is a little lower than Canada's, but from the European point of view these two countries are much lower than the countries of Western Europe.

Professor Kragh went on to say: "I might finish by saying, perhaps, that we do not consider a price increase of a couple of per cent very dangerous in Sweden, in any event because we have had this record of experience without very much happening really. And when I talk about very much happening, I mean the external balance." And finally, "I would like to stress that the reason we have not been so very occupied or alarmed before, is that we have not had any troubles with external matters and even now have not had any drain on our foreign exchange reserves and that is the criteria that the wages have not been rising too fast. When we are in trouble with foreign exchange we will be really alarmed as to prices."

In Europe generally, with the exception of Germany, the main constraint for much of the time on the simultaneous achievement of the various goals has been the balance of payments. Within the room permitted by this constraint, the governments of these countries have pursued vigorous policies for high employment and rapid growth but have experienced persistent and significant increases in prices.

In North America, the goal of price stability has had a considerably higher priority. There has been a greater sensitivity to the unequal impacts, the inequities, and the distortions from persistently rising prices, resulting in a distinctly lesser degree of emphasis on the attainment of very low rates of unemployment and very high rates of sustained growth.

In spite of the very considerable concern over prices in the United States and Canada during the postwar period, there has been a good deal of frustration over what has taken place. There have been substantial increases relieved from time to time by periods of relative stability when economic growth was slow. Since the war price and cost developments in the two countries have been pervaded, and in large measure dominated, by a phenomenon about which we know relatively little: the persistent upward drift in the rapidly expanding service sector of the economy. The general level of service prices has been rising about twice as fast as that of goods prices, according to the measurements we are now using. The value of output in the service sector is more than half of the total output of the economy. The overwhelming proportion of all the new jobs which have appeared over the past twenty years, something like four-fifths have arisen in the service industries. About three-quarters of all professional and technical workers are now engaged in the service industries. We have become a service-oriented economy. The service sector is where most of the new employment takes place, where consumer and government expenditures are rising most rapidly, where costs are rising most steadily, and where increases in productivity appear to be substantially lower than in the relatively declining goods sector. This is surely a noteworthy circumstance, but our information is relatively poor. We do not know very much about what is really happening and even less about the significance of these trends for the general development of costs and prices in the economy. If we are to gain a good perspective of our problem, we shall have to study in more depth this rapidly growing area of economic activity where our information is skimpy and our measurements are deficient.

Another matter about which our information is much less than satisfactory is that relating to the effects of the exercise of market power by large corporations and trade unions. The unavoidably brief survey which we were able to make of the available evidence did not indicate that market power as such had any substantial general influence one way or the other on the upward movements of prices and costs over the short run. An examination of the available evidence suggests that the consequences of the exercise of market power are of primary significance for the longer run with regard to costs, income distribution, and the allocation of resources. Of course, these longer-run implications could be very important and they call for a much more thorough study.

The environment of North America is a matter of basic importance for Canadian experience. Because of the massive economic interdependence of Canada and the United States, Canadian goals concerning prices, costs, and rates of economic growth are inevitably very strongly affected by those which prevail south of the border. Any examination of price movements in the two countries, whether for a relatively short period of two or three years, or for a period as long as half a century, will reveal a remarkable correspondence in both the range and speed of movement. As a result of this circumstance, the Economic Council, in its *Third Annual Review*, observed this relation:

The power of the underlying forces making for longer-term similarity of price movements in the two countries is apparent. Given these conditions, it is clearly not realistic for Canada to aim at a price performance that is very different, either in upward or downward direction, from the parallel performance in the United States. Barring a large and continuous offsetting movement in the exchange rate, or the deliberate insulation of the whole economy on a scale and at a cost that few Canadians would be prepared to tolerate, an attempt to do very much better, or very much worse, than the United States in achieving reasonable price stability would not be sound policy (p. 56).

Of course, this does not mean that what happens in the United States must always be accepted, and that there is nothing for Canada to do. In the first place, it may not be easy to do much better, but it is quite possible to do much worse. Any persistent rise in prices and costs out of line with those in the United States will bring trouble with the balance of payments. When this happens, we face either an adjustment of the exchange rate, which cannot be used as a continuous medicine, or we face adjustments which are very likely to bring unemployment and slow growth. In such circumstances, we would fail to achieve any of our economic goals. Monetary and fiscal policies designed to maintain high levels of demand and rapid expansion must be accompanied by large and sustained improvements in productivity if we are to avoid, for very long, the constraint imposed by the balance of payments in a North American environment, where there is a high sensitivity to inflationary pressures.

Within the framework of the external relations under which we have to operate, there are a number of particular circumstances with which Canadian policy-makers must cope. Not only is there a high degree of interdependence between the Canadian and American economies, but the interdependence operates in a way which in a number of respects poses special problems for Canada.

It has been said that "when the United States sneezes Canada gets pneumonia." Recently some one has added the remark that "when the United States has a slight fever, Canada becomes delirious." There is a great deal of truth in these analogies. This truth affects very greatly the problem of achieving our economic goals and of resolving the conflicts between them. There is a very close correspondence in the economic fluctuations in the two countries. While the business cycles move quite closely together, the Canadian economy tends to be more volatile. There have been exceptions to this broad generalization, but not recently. Among several factors which account for this, there are one or two which could be mentioned: changes in the levels of American economic activity tend to bring about a relatively larger proportionate change in Canadian exports to that country, and a strong growth of exports to the United States always has a very stimulating effect on Canadian expansion. The rapid growth of demand for Canadian exports from that huge market can bump very quickly up against Canadian capacity. And this in turn may bring about new waves of capital expansion. Of course, the opposite happens when the US business cycle turns down.

The second matter of importance is the fact that the construction industry is a considerably larger part of the total Canadian economy than is the construction industry in the United States. The wide swings in this important sector of the Canadian economy are a source of considerable instability in Canadian prices and costs. The greater volatility of the Canadian economy arising from these and other factors poses a number of particular problems for Canadian policy.

While we seem to have been able to overcome the curse of massive unemployment, we have not yet overcome the business cycle—at least not in North America. Since the war, cyclical fluctuations have been relatively mild, but they have not disappeared. Here again there is a very close correspondence between the movements of cycles in Canada and the movements of the cycles in the United States. I need hardly say which of the two countries is the principal culprit, if there is a culprit. For better or for worse, the US business cycle gets reflected in the Canadian economy as do the typical movements in wages, prices, profits, and employment. Canadian policy has to cope with them. If we are concerned about the relationships we would like to see exist between wages, prices, profits, and levels of employment, we have to have in mind which stage of the business cycle we are in. Where economic growth proceeds in a cyclical fashion, and even if the cycles are relatively mild, these relationships, or these trade-offs or whatever you want to call them, are not fixed. They change according to the stage of the cycle. Analysts have pointed out that these movements and relationships are affected by a number of important leads and lags.

Typically, there is a tendency in the early stages of a business-cycle recovery for profits to move up relatively rapidly and for wages and prices to lag. In the important manufacturing industry, in particular, at that stage of the cycle, unit profits tend to rise and unit wages tend to fall, while productivity is advancing rapidly. As the top of the cycle is reached, there is an acceleration in the rate of increase of wages and prices, because unemployment falls to relatively low levels and unit profits tend to contract. After the peak of the cycle is passed, prices and unit wage costs may continue to increase for some time, while investment falls off and unemployment begins to increase. Later, as the cycle continues in its downward phase, the rate of price and wage increases slackens off. As long as we have business cycles, even if they are relatively mild, we have to keep in mind the leads and lags which are likely to be present at any particular time. This circumstance presents considerable problems of timing for public policy, and makes it dangerous to generalize about the relevance or inevitability of certain relationships that may exist at a particular time.

A wise and very successful friend of mine once remarked to me: "When I see an announcement of an official inquiry into high prices, then I know it is time to buy bonds." My own observations have confirmed the shrewdness of this statement. The leads and lags which appear to be typical of postwar North American business cycles have also other implications for public policy, because actions of policy cannot be expected to be effective without some considerable delays. Because of this there is always the danger of ill-timed measures which are designed to deal with situations that have already passed.

Given all these general influences, and the basic environment in which we exist in this country, what can we say about some of the particular goals and objectives of public policy? What about the goals concerning employment and prices? In its *First Annual Review*, the Economic Council concluded "that a 97 per cent rate of employment, or a 3 per cent rate of unemployment for the labour force, would constitute a realistic objective to be aimed at over the balance of the 1960's, and that economic policy should be actively directed to the achievement of this target" (p. 38).

I want to emphasize in particular that this objective was to be achieved, in the view of the Council, over a period of time, and that it was to be pursued not simply by the use of appropriate monetary and fiscal policies, but by a combination of complementary economic policies in other fields as well. In this connection, the Council stated explicitly: "We believe that this potential level of the utilization of the labour force can be achieved on a sustained basis only if effective labour market policies are developed to promote higher and more efficient use of our manpower resources" (*First Annual Review*, p. 38). The Council has placed a strong emphasis in its reports and recommendations on the development of an adequate manpower programme and on other programmes to improve supplies and productivity in order to minimize the frictional and structural impediments to a high employment policy.

Commenting on the objective of reasonable price stability the Council "assumed that if annual average rates of changes in prices and costs to 1970 can be contained within the limits of the ranges of movements over the decade from 1953 to 1963, this would represent the attainment of a satisfactory degree of price and cost stability." In this period the general indexes ranged within limits of 1½ to 2 per cent a year. The Council felt "it should be emphasized that a continuation of this performance into the future [would] undoubtedly be a difficult task to achieve, especially under the high demand and high employment conditions which we have postulated." Because of this anticipated difficulty, the Council called for policies and programmes which were designed to achieve a more rapid growth in productivity, increased international competition, increased adjustment to change and mobility of productive resources through better labour-market policies, and more long-term planning of capital investment in business. The Council also advocated longer-term planning and greater stability in the rate of growth of government expenditures. In the view of the Council, the achievement of the price goal and the active implementation of effective programmes in all these areas of private and public policy were closely linked. Needless to say, a favourable international environment was recognized as the indispensable requirement for the attainment of virtually every Canadian goal.

In summary, if we wish to view the problem in perspective, we must view it in the context of the influences which invariably and inevitably play upon us from abroad and in the context of a whole range of complementary policies and programmes which can be followed at home. One can say that we have set ambitious goals for our economy. Moreover, we are asking for high standards of performance in the achievement of each and every one of these goals. This has proven to be very difficult to effect. There has been some considerable success but it remains a task which presents dilemmas, conflicts, and difficult choices. In the search for answers it is not surprising that there is a temptation to look for some simple all-embracing formula.

A DIAGNOSIS
OF THE PROBLEM

INTRODUCTION, *by W. Donald Wood*

The diagnostic focus of the papers in this section is appropriate at this stage, because one of the most important first steps in formulating economic policy is to develop a clear picture of objectives and the problems to be solved. Once the problems have been clearly defined, it is easier to develop effective policy instruments to achieve our goals.

Unfortunately, most economic issues are exceedingly complex and do not yield to simple, unqualified answers. Moreover, the weight given to different public policy goals also depends on economic and social philosophy; hence, many of our objectives cannot be considered absolute, and society is constantly working out through practical compromises the "best" balance among conflicting and changing objectives. The task of public economic policy has been further complicated in recent decades as governments have shouldered increasing responsibilities in many areas of economic affairs.

One of the most important and clearest statements of Canada's main economic goals was set forth by the Economic Council of Canada in its *First Annual Review*: "The main purpose of this Review is to examine the problem of achieving simultaneously and consistently certain basic economic and social goals in the Canadian economy in the medium-term future, specifically, over the next five years to 1970. These goals . . . may be stated briefly as follows: full employment; a high rate of economic growth; reasonable stability of prices; a viable balance of payments; and an equitable distribution of rising incomes" (p. 1).

I believe there has been a consensus in Canada regarding the desirability of these broad goals; there may be some differences over specific aspects and about the specific measures needed to achieve these objectives. The sharper debate centres more on the question of whether these goals can be achieved simultaneously, particularly price stability and full employment. There are those who take the position that there is a definite conflict between these policy objectives, supporting their argument with empirical studies that indicate there is a high degree of correlation between high rates of price increases and lower rates of unemployment, and between lower rates of price increases and higher rates of unemployment, which necessitates some "trade off" between these two policy objectives.

The trade-off thesis has been challenged, however, by some who believe these objectives are reasonably compatible. They argue that it is dangerous to interpret rigid trade-off empirical relationships from the past as a guide for the present. It is also felt that the apparent conflicts between a low employment rate and stable prices can be substantially reduced by measures such as improved knowledge about our economic problems, a more appropriate mix of policies, better specific policy devices, and an improvement in economic adjustment mechanisms.

In brief these are the broad questions and issues which Professor Reuber and Mr. McQueen will discuss.

Stable Prices, High Employment, and Economic Growth: Must Canada Choose?

GRANT L. REUBER

Most of us in our everyday lives have been faced with the difficulty of choosing among several goals, all of which are highly desirable in themselves, but each of which is inconsistent with some of the others to some degree. In this situation it is impossible fully to achieve each objective. A simple example of such a dilemma is the conflict of the desire for income which requires effort, and the desire for leisure. Few of us opt for all work or all leisure. Most of us elect a compromise: some income and some leisure. In this sense we can say that we are willing to trade-off income against leisure.

Nations confront similar difficulties in choosing among the objectives of economic policy. Nowadays governments in most, if not all, countries aspire to a wide range of economic goals: full employment, stable prices, rapid and sustained economic growth, balance-of-payments equilibrium, wide regional dispersion of economic development, and greater equality of income, wealth, and opportunity, to mention only a few. If it were merely a matter of compiling a list of desirable goals, questions of economic policy would be comparatively simple. However, if these various goals conflict with each other to some extent, compiling such a list is only the first step in formulating satisfactory policies. If all goals cannot be attained simultaneously, a hard choice must be made about how far to pursue one objective at the expense of others. In this situation most policy-makers, analogous to most individuals, can be expected to elect a compromise, trading off some portion of one objective so as not to fall further short on some other.

This paper focuses on three key objectives of Canadian economic policy: high employment, price stability, and economic growth. The basic question which is directly posed is "How great is the degree of conflict between these policy objectives?" To try to answer this question it is necessary to evaluate the interrelations of these objectives empirically and to consider the policy implications of the empirical evidence.

The underlying economic forces generating increases in prices may be conveniently grouped into two broad and interdependent categories: changes in costs on the supply side and changes in demand.

On the supply side by far the largest cost of production is composed of wages and salaries. In 1965 labour income made up two-thirds of net factor cost. Given the importance of labour costs, it is evident that changes in wages and salaries can have an important influence on Canadian price levels.

How important this influence will be will depend in part on changes in productivity, i.e., economic growth. If wages generally increase by about the same rate as the increase in productivity, then the increase in wages will not exert much of an upward pressure on prices, since unit labour costs will not increase. Indeed, if increases in productivity exceed increases in wages, it is conceivable that prices may decline at the same time that wages are rising, since in this case unit labour costs will be falling.

A third important cost factor to be considered is the cost of imported goods and services which in recent years have been equal to almost one-quarter of our gross national expenditure. Because of their relative size, it is apparent that increases in import prices can exert important upward pressure on Canadian prices. In this connection, it should be noted that changes in import prices may arise from changes in prices in the countries where our imports originate—mainly the United States—or from changes in Canada's foreign exchange, e.g., the depreciation of the Canadian dollar in 1961–62.

A fourth important cost factor to be considered in trying to explain *current* price changes is the lagged effect of changes in costs and prices in an earlier period. The full effect of a change in costs today will not be immediately reflected in prices. Only after a period of time will the full effect of the change in costs have percolated through the economy and have become fully reflected in prices. For example, the full effect on prices of the exchange depreciation of 1961–62 was not fully reflected in Canadian prices in 1962; it took considerable time for the increase in import prices resulting from the depreciation to be fully reflected in consumer prices.

The extent to which changes in costs are passed on in the form of higher prices depends on demand conditions. It is conceivable, for example, that in a situation where there is considerable excess capacity in the economy, increases in costs will be largely absorbed in lower profits and rents and will have little or no effect on prices. On the other hand, when demand conditions permit, increases in costs may be fully passed on in the form of higher prices. And beyond this point, demand may be so strong as not only to make it feasible to pass on cost increases, but also to induce increases in profits and rents as well as further increases in labour and other costs. Thus, a self-generating process may become established in which rising costs tend to induce increases in prices, which in turn tend to induce increases in costs.

This, very briefly, is the traditional picture of the inflationary process. The emphasis is on the level of aggregate demand as the prime factor influencing the stability of prices and costs. The implied policy implication is that by skilfully regulating the level of total demand through monetary and fiscal policy, price stability can be achieved, particularly in an economy experiencing substantial growth in productivity, and the economy can simultaneously operate at full employment. From the standpoint of economic policy, the main problem is to avoid excess aggregate demand and over-full employment through the skilful deployment of monetary and fiscal policies. In an economy experiencing substantial gains in productivity the traditional picture suggests little, if any, conflict between the objectives of price stability and full employment.

This picture can be readily extended to take into account the openness of the Canadian economy. The balance of payments will be in equilibrium at full employment, given the appropriate level of the exchange rate and appropriate monetary and fiscal policies. If equilibrium is not attained at this point, adjustments in the exchange rate as well as in the mix of monetary and fiscal policy are called for.

Although most, if not all, economists are quite prepared to grant the importance of aggregate demand as a factor influencing prices, this traditional picture of the inflationary process has been intensively re-examined during the past decade. This re-examination was stimulated in part by experience in North America and elsewhere in the late fifties and early sixties when prices continued to rise in the face of high levels of unemployment and significant unused capacity. In the course of this re-examination some economists gave considerable emphasis to the influence of costs in pushing up prices. In brief, the "cost-push" view is that sellers set their prices simply by adding up their costs and adding an appropriate mark-up for profits based on past experience or tradition. As costs rise, the increases are largely passed along in the form of higher prices. This is possible since governments nowadays are politically committed to full employment and consequently are bound to pursue monetary and fiscal policies which will accommodate the increase in prices required to absorb the increase in costs. Failure to provide such accommodation would result in an unacceptable level of unemployment. Aware of the government's commitment to full employment, neither labour in their demands nor management in their concessions are deterred by the prospect that the results of their agreements may lead to higher prices, thereby seriously impairing both employment and profits.

This view of the inflationary process emphasizes the market power of unions and big business to raise wages at their discretion and assumes a political environment in which governments are incapable of allowing market conditions to arise which will discipline these powerful groups. In these circumstances, little hope is held out for the traditional instruments of monetary and fiscal policy. Instead, it is suggested that more reliance must be placed on direct measures of various kinds, some of which may be general in character and some of which may be selective.

The cost-push view of the inflationary process is more complex when the openness of the Canadian economy is taken into account. This is because adverse changes in the balance of payments induced by rising domestic costs and prices may greatly strengthen the will and the ability of the authorities to restrain domestic demand. This factor, however, may not be as important as sometimes suggested for at least two reasons. For one thing, this balance-of-payments constraint may not prove very effective if prices abroad are rising at about the same pace as at home. For another, this constraint can be relaxed by allowing the exchange rate to depreciate or by inducing greater inflows of capital. Although one may question whether the authorities would be prepared to countenance a more-or-less continuous exchange depreciation or an accelerating inflow of foreign capital in order to accommodate domestic price inflation, they may nevertheless be prepared to accept such policies long enough to give rise to lengthy periods of rising prices.

One difficulty with the cost-push thesis is, of course, that it does not really explain why prices rise at the rate they do. If powerful groups can set their incomes without taking demand into account, why do they raise their incomes at the rate they do rather than at some higher rate? Secondly, one may question whether the ability of governments to resist cost increases generated by private groups with market power is as weak as assumed. Governments have, after all, survived at the polls in spite of increases in taxes, deferment of expenditures, and the sanctioning of very tight money. Despite these qualifications, this cost-push picture of price inflation has consider-able plausibility for a mixed economy such as ours. Rising prices cannot simply be dismissed as a phenomenon of excess demand which can be fully remedied through traditional monetary and fiscal measures.

There are two reasons for outlining these two views of the inflationary process. One is that there has been considerable popular as well as professional discussion of the relative weights to be given to these two views in explaining rising prices in North America and Western Europe. The other is that between them, these views highlight the factors which can be considered important in explain-ing rising prices. The difference between the two views can be readily illustrated graphically.[1] In figure 1 the percentage rate of

[1]Figure one is drawn on the assumptions of no change in productivity and no lags.

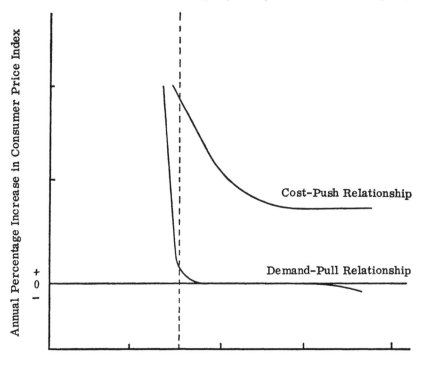

Unemployment as Percentage of Labour Force

FIG. 1. Hypothetical illustration of cost-push and demand-pull interpretations of
the relationship between unemployment and price change.

change in prices is plotted on the vertical axis and the unemployment percentage, representing the degree of excess capacity in the
economy, is plotted along the horizontal axis. One hypothetical
curve illustrates the type of price-change–unemployment relationship suggested by the demand-pull view of inflation. At very low
levels of unemployment prices rise sharply; at unemployment levels
above the full-employment level, prices are stable (but rigid down-
wards). The other hypothetical curve illustrates the type of price-
change–unemployment relationship suggested by the cost-push view
of inflation. At very low levels of unemployment prices increase
sharply in response to excess demand; prices continue to rise at a
substantial rate even when unemployment levels are high. Thus,
the difference between these views can be thought of in terms of
the empirical question of what is the shape and position of the

curve showing the actual relationship between the rate of increase in consumer prices and the level of unemployment. The answer to this question would serve to identify the degree of conflict between the policy goals of high employment and price stability.

Before attempting to answer this empirical question, a few comments are called for regarding the third key objective of economic policy with which we are concerned: the rate of economic growth. For our purposes the term economic growth is defined as the rate of productivity growth, where productivity is defined as output per man-hour. The issue in hand is whether the secular rate of productivity growth is responsive to the rate of change in prices and the level of unemployment, abstracting from short-term cyclical changes. As a broad generalization, it can be said that the theoretical literature in economics gives some presumption in favour of two views on this issue.

The first view, based on classical economics, is that the secular rate of productivity growth is independent of the rate of change in prices and the level of unemployment. The rate of growth, on classical assumptions, is determined by real factors, such as consumer preferences, the quantity and quality of factor inputs, and enterprise. Abstracting from cyclical deviations, the economy is assumed to be fully employed. The second view, the most brilliant early exposition of which is to be found in J. M. Keynes's *A Treatise on Money*, is that the rate of productivity growth is positively correlated with high employment and moderately rising prices. There are several reasons why one might expect to find such a positive association: (*i*) the volume of voluntary saving and capital formation can be expected to be greater with higher levels of employment and income than with the lower levels of employment and income; (*ii*) rising prices act as a tax on fixed income groups and others who fail to maintain their real incomes in the face of rising prices; the forced savings thus generated add further to capital formation and hence productivity; (*iii*) labour mobility, as well as the mobility of other scarce factors, is likely to be greater when demand is high and factor prices are rising; (*iv*) rising prices tend to undermine the dampening influence of legal and institutional restrictions on productivity growth, e.g., the dampening effect on growth of laws setting unrealistically high minimum wages may be eroded by rising prices; and (*v*) a high level of demand is likely to enhance the development and introduction of technical innovations and cost-reducing practices. Once more, the issue boils down to an empirical question.

I might add finally that, as I read it at least, neither the theoretical nor the empirical literature in economics gives much reason for believing that over the long run the rate of productivity growth is negatively correlated with high employment and moderately rising prices. The main argument I can find in favour of this proposition suggests that higher unemployment reduces job security and profits, which in turn induces the community to work harder, to seek out cheaper methods of production, and so forth. It seems implausible to me that the totality of all the factors tending to increase productivity when the economy is run at full capacity do not have at least as stimulating an effect on productivity as the purgative of unemployment.

The empirical evidence which I am about to present on the questions raised above is based mainly on research on which I and three of my colleagues have been engaged for some time. Our most recent work in this area was done for the Economic Council of Canada.[2]

I should like to begin this review of the empirical evidence by asserting four basic conclusions which seem to be indicated by our evidence:

(1) Within the range of experience in this country, there is little or no evidence that the secular rate of productivity growth in Canada is significantly affected by the level of unemployment or the rate of price increase (abstracting from cyclical changes). Slight traces can be found in the statistics of a positive association between the secular rate of productivity growth and high levels of employment and rising prices; but the evidence is impressionistic

[2]Ronald G. Bodkin, Elizabeth P. Bond, Grant L. Reuber, and T. Russell Robinson, *Price Stability and High Employment: The Options for Canadian Economic Policy*. Special Study No. 5. Prepared for the Economic Council of Canada (Ottawa: Queen's Printer, 1967). G. L. Reuber, "The Objectives of Canadian Monetary Policy, 1949–61: Empirical 'Trade-Offs' and the Reaction Function of the Authorities," *Journal of Political Economy* LXXII (April 1964) 109–32; *The Objectives of Monetary Policy*. Working Paper prepared for the Royal Commission on Banking and Finance, mimeo (Ottawa: Queen's Printer, 1962). Ronald G. Bodkin, "An Analysis of the Trade-Offs Between Full Employment, Price Stability and Other Economic Goals," in S. F. Kaliski, ed., *Canadian Economic Policy Since the War* (Montreal: Private Planning Association, 1966); *The Wage-Price-Productivity Nexus* (Philadelphia: University of Pennsylvania Press, 1966).

and certainly fails to support the hypothesis of a strong and significant positive relationship. This conclusion for Canada coincides with the findings of a substantial number of studies which have considered this relationship for the United States and other countries.[3]

(2) There is strong evidence that within the range of unemployment rates and price-level changes relevant to public policy discussions in this country, the level of employment and degree of price stability in the country are inversely related. In other words, there is strong evidence of a conflict between the objectives of high employment and price stability. Significant evidence of such a conflict exists for other industrialized countries as well. No evidence has been found for Canada, nor for any other country, to suggest that within the range of experience under consideration these two objectives are either independent of each other or are complementary.

(3) There is equally strong evidence that the relationship between the level of unemployment and the rate of change in prices in Canada is greatly complicated by the openness of the Canadian economy and the magnitude and pervasiveness of the influence of foreign (especially US) price and wage changes on Canadian wages and prices. Given the importance of this external influence and given the limitations on public policy, it is unlikely that price changes in Canada can deviate very much from price changes in the United States, particularly if Canada adheres to a fixed foreign exchange rate.

(4) The empirical evidence for Canada indicates that profits per unit of output have some positive influence on the rate of price change via the influence of unit profits on the rate of change in wages. This, however, is relatively weaker than the influence of unemployment and foreign prices on price changes.

Little more will be said about the first of these conclusions. It may be noted in passing that perhaps one reason why the secular rate of growth does not appear to be positively influenced by high employment and rising prices is because the public may adjust

---

[3]Economists in the past have given considerable attention to the empirical effect on the rate of economic growth of the level of unemployment and the degree of price stability. See, for example, the publications cited in Reuber, *The Objectives of Monetary Policy*, 89.

more readily than might be expected to the general environment of employment and price-level changes in which it finds itself. This adjustment is reflected not only directly in thousands of private market transactions, but also indirectly in the policies which the public demands of its government, e.g., in the field of social security.

Our estimate of the relationship between the rate of change in prices and the level of unemployment is a derived relationship. It is based upon two directly estimated relationships. The first is a "wage-adjustment" relationship showing the relation between the level of unemployment and the rate of change in wages; and the second is a "price-change" relationship indicating the relation between the rate of change in wages and the rate of change in prices. Both are based on quarterly data for the 1953–65 period.

The estimated wage-adjustment relationship indicates that about 85 per cent of the variation in the rate of change in money wages from 1953 to 1965 can be explained by variations in (*i*) the rate of unemployment, (*ii*) the rate of change in consumer prices, (*iii*) the rate of change in US wages, (*iv*) the rate of change in wages in the previous year, and (*v*) the *level* of profits per unit of output in manufacturing. This list of significant factors influencing the rate of increase in wages contains few, if any, surprises. It is generally recognized that as labour becomes scarcer and scarcer, wages are likely to rise at an accelerating rate. Similarly, it is widely accepted that wage demands will be stronger the more rapid the increase in the cost of living and the higher the level of profits. Moreover, the higher the level of profits the easier it seems likely to be for employers to accede to wage demands. The role of lags is also as expected: wage demands today are likely to be influenced by what happened to wages a year ago.

Less obvious is the role which US wages seem to play in determining Canadian wages. It has frequently been suggested that the policies of Canadian trade unions are influenced by the policies of US unions with which some Canadian unions have close relationships. Moreover, Canadian labour has sometimes expressed its wage demands in relation to US wages, usually demanding parity with US wages now or over a period of time. In addition, Canadian wages may be influenced by US wages in much the same way that wages in many US industries seem to be influenced by wages in a "key group" of US industries. Some evidence has accumulated to suggest that in the US wage settlements in the key group set the pace which other wage settlements tend to follow.[4] For Canada, the key group of settlements to which wages may be geared may be wages in the US rather than in some domestic sector.

Our estimated price-change relationship for the same period indicated that about 87 per cent of the variation in the rate of change in prices can be explained by a constant term and variations in (*i*) the rate of change in wages, (*ii*) the rate of change in import prices, and (*iii*) the rate of change in prices in the past. This list of significant factors influencing the rate of increase in prices also contains few surprises.

By combining the estimated wage-adjustment and price-change relationships, a third relationship can be derived from which can be directly calculated the trade-offs between the rate of price change and the level of unemployment. In order to calculate these trade-offs, we make two assumptions. First, we abstract from lags in the adjustment of prices and wages to current economic conditions. In effect, this means that our estimates try to answer the question: What will be the relationship between the current level of unemployment and the current rate of price change after enough time has elapsed for all lags in the economy to have worked themselves out fully? Secondly, the trade-offs between unemployment and the rate of price change will be conditioned by what is happening to the other variables which influence prices. Consequently, such trade-offs can only be estimated by holding these other variables fixed at some predetermined levels.

For present purposes two sets of assumptions are made about the values of these other variables. One set postulates a "non-inflationary" environment in which import prices remain unchanged, US wages rise at a rate which is held to be consistent with stable US prices, and unit profits are at a level equal to their average level from 1953 to 1965. The second set of assumptions assumes an "inflationary" environment in which import prices rise at 2 per cent

[4]O. Eckstein and T. A. Wilson, "The Determination of Money Wages in American Industry," *Quarterly Journal of Economics* LXXVI (August 1962), 379–414.

per year, US wages rise at 6 per cent per year, and unit profits are half way between their peak and average values for the 1953–65 period. The estimated trade-off relationships based on these assumptions are given in table 1 and are shown graphically in figure 2.

Consider first the estimates based on the assumption of a non-inflationary environment. On this assumption it appears reasonable to expect the Canadian price level to remain constant when the unemployment rate is about 4¾ per cent. When unemployment falls to 2½ per cent, prices can be expected to rise by about 4 per cent per year. When unemployment rises to 8 per cent per year prices can be expected to fall by 1 per cent per year.

The picture changes sharply when an inflationary environment is assumed. In this situation there is no level of unemployment that is consistent with stable prices. At a 4 per cent level of unemployment retail prices can be expected to rise by 5 per cent; at a 2½ per cent level of unemployment retail prices can be expected to rise by more than 8 per cent; and when unemployment is 8 per cent prices are likely to rise by about 3½ per cent. In short, if foreign prices are rising by about 2 per cent per year, Canadian prices can be expected to rise substantially even at levels of unemployment that are well beyond anything that is politically tolerable.

Trade-off measurements are, of course, only approximations. At best they are measures of central tendency. They are subject to all the limitations of the data on which they are based as well as to the technical limitations of the methods employed. This said, it needs

TABLE 1

ESTIMATED PRICE-CHANGE-UNEMPLOYMENT TRADE-OFFS, 1953–65

Unemployment as percentage of labour force	Annual percentage change in consumer price index	
	Non-inflationary environment assumptions	Inflationary environment assumptions
2.5	3.9	8.3
3.0	2.2	6.7
4.0	0.6	5.0
5.0	−0.2	4.2
6.0	−0.6	3.8
7.0	−0.9	3.6
8.0	−1.0	3.4

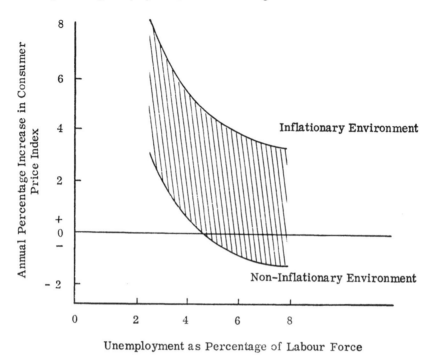

FIG. 2. Estimated trade-offs between unemployment and price change, 1953–65.

to be emphasized that virtually every other method of ascertaining how the economy works is subject to the same limitations as the econometric techniques used for this analysis, and econometric methods, in contrast to casual empiricism, have the great advantage of lending themselves to at least some objective testing.

An additional qualification to be noted is that the estimates are based on Canada's economic experience from 1953–65. Their relevance to circumstances outside this range of experience is uncertain. This is an inevitable difficulty which, failing controlled experiments, bedevils all discussions of economic policy. Two points can, however, be made on behalf of the estimates just presented. First, the period upon which the estimates are based encompasses quite a diverse range of economic circumstances with respect to the range of domestic and foreign price and wage changes, the level of unemployment, the postures of economic policy, the changes in the structure of the economy, the rate of economic growth, the pattern of economic instability, the variation in expectations, and so forth. Secondly, the estimates stand up well when examined in the light of estimates made of Canada's experience over the last forty years as well as of postwar experience in other countries. In technical language, the estimates gave evidence of only mild instability when put through a series of fairly stiff statistical tests. These estimates can probably be relied upon with at least as much confidence as is warranted by most of the knowledge of the economy which is necessarily relied upon for purposes of evaluating and formulating policies.

The title of this paper poses the question of whether Canada must choose between the goals of stable prices, high employment, and economic growth. Even after full allowance is made for all the qualifications, the evidence leaves little doubt that there is a conflict between the goals of price stability and full employment, and that Canadians inevitably must choose how much of one goal they are prepared to sacrifice in the interests of more fully achieving the other. The evidence on the relationship between long-run economic growth and price stability and the level of employment is less clear, but seems to indicate that the long-run rate of growth is largely independent of the price and employment objectives within the range of experience relevant to policy discussion in this country. This suggests that Canadians do not have to choose between the objective of economic growth and the other two objectives of policy; their choice between the goals of price stability and high employment can be expected to have little if any influence on the long-run economic growth of the country.

The conclusion that the long-run rate of economic growth is largely independent of the general level of unemployment and the rate of price inflation has at least two important policy implications. For one thing, it suggests that it only muddies the waters of public discussion and hampers the achievement of good economic policy for anyone to suggest that low levels of unemployment, by the standards of our experience, and the concomitant increases in prices are inimical to the long-run economic growth of this country. At worst, there seems to be no relation between the rate of growth and the level of employment, and there may in fact be a weak and only dimly perceptible positive relationship. In addition, this conclusion about the growth objective suggests that in formulating general monetary and fiscal policies in this country for stabilization purposes, the authorities should keep their eyes firmly glued on the performance of the economy in terms of employment and price level changes and should not allow themselves to be misled by the illusion that higher unemployment and more stable prices than we have experienced recently will promote the long-run economic growth of this country.

Turning to the choice between price stability and high employment, one should think first of all in terms of what policies might be adopted to reduce the degree of conflict between these two goals. What can be done to shift the trade-off curve downward and to the left, closer to the axes? The slope and position of the trade-off curve reflect the underlying structural elements of the economy, e.g., its resource base, the attitudes of the public, its institutional arrangements (particularly its labour market and price-setting mechanisms), and its international relationships. It also reflects the number of policy instruments available for use, their impact on the economic structure, and the interrelations of the various instruments of policy. Within this context one may think in terms of policies designed to achieve greater competition in product and factor markets and a higher mobility of labour and other factors between regions and occupations. For example, to the extent that the labour market policies advocated by the Economic Council in its *Second Annual Review* prove effective, these policies will result in a shift in the trade-off curve closer to the axes. Similarly, "incomes policies," as used in the United States and a number of European countries, can be thought of as attempts to shift the trade-off curve to a more favourable position.

Although it may be possible to reduce the degree of conflict between full employment and price stability through such policies, experience in Canada and elsewhere gives little reason for believing that this conflict can be reduced to the point where it ceases to be important for public policy. Thus, the country seems inevitably to be faced with the question of choosing the point on the trade-off curve which is least disadvantageous. Having made its choice, the country faces the further policy question of how to regulate the aggregate level of demand by means of general monetary and fiscal policies in order to achieve this optimum combination.

What is the optimum combination of unemployment and price change at which stabilization policy should aim? In order to answer this, an assessment of the relative costs of price inflation and unemployment is required. This poses difficult questions about which we know only too little and which continue to receive less attention than they deserve. Moreover, important considerations of political and social policy are raised. The issue is nevertheless unavoidable. Anyone who, for example, suggests that demand should be dampened in the interests of greater price stability is implicitly suggesting that the benefits from greater price stability will outweigh the costs of the higher unemployment associated with greater price stability. Similarly, anyone who advocates an expansion in demand implies that the gains from the resulting reduction in unemployment will outweigh the costs of the associated increase in the rate of price increase.

It is not possible to explore this matter at any length here. I leave aside all political and social considerations, fully recognizing that they may be very important. The economic costs of unemployment and price inflation can be usefully grouped into two categories: those related to the total real output of the community, and those related to the distribution of income and wealth. With regard to the first category, one of the principal costs of unemployment consists of the output foregone as a result of failing to employ productively all the labour, willing and able to work at prevailing wages. To the extent that high employment stimulates productivity growth, further costs in terms of output foregone arise as the level of unemployment is allowed to rise. For the economy as a whole, a principal cost of moderate inflation arises from the reduction in the usefulness of money. Under inflationary conditions, there will be a tendency to hold a higher proportion of wealth in the form of real goods, which are produced at a cost, in place of money, which is virtually costless to produce. Taking into account only these aggregative real costs and assuming no balance-of-payments constraint, estimates have been made of the price-change–unemployment combination for which the incremental cost of unemployment is approximately equal to the incremental cost of price inflation. These estimates should be regarded as extremely rough and tentative approximations. They do suggest, however, that it may be feasible to run the economy at quite a high level of employment, by the historical standards of this country, before the aggregative costs of inflation begin to outweigh, on the margin, the costs of inflation.

It is even more difficult to say what the optimum combination is when one takes into account distributive costs. Several points should be noted in this connection. First and foremost, it is high time that the distributive effects of unemployment are taken into account, as well as the distributive effects of price inflation, when this question is considered. Distributive justice is no less important when inequities arise from unemployment than from price changes. Few would agree that the interests of bond holders, pensioners, and fixed-income groups should be given priority over the interests of the older and the very young workers, minority groups, those who are less skilled and less healthy, those living in the more remote areas of the country, and those running small businesses: those groups upon whom the incidence of unemployment is greatest. Secondly, the empirical studies that have been made of the distributive effects of price inflation suggest that these are much less than usually suggested.[5] This is because the public learns from past experience and before long begins to allow for future price increases in its contractual arrangements. Interest rates on bonds, for example, are adjusted upward to reflect the expected decline in the purchasing power of the fixed value of bonds. Since the First World War retail prices in North America in every year have been higher than in the previous year with only ten exceptions, nine of these occurring during the interwar period. No one can claim that price increases are a recent phenomenon being sprung on the public unexpectedly. In the light of the past and with the commitment of the country to a mixed economy and the goal of full employment, can anyone claim an injustice if he bets on price stability in the future and loses? Is there anyone in the country who, in fact, seriously believes that prices will not continue to increase in coming years? And in the light of experience, is there any reason for

[5]Reuber, *The Objectives of Monetary Policy*, chap. v.

[6]*Ibid.* Discussions on this question frequently imply an inconsistency: at the same time that it is argued that price inflation has serious distributive effects, it is also argued or implied that after a time the public will generally come to expect inflation and will adapt to it.

believing that a continuous mild upward movement in prices cannot be sustained and is inevitably doomed to deteriorate into hyper-inflation?

In addition to these considerations, it should be recognized that most governments nowadays actively redistribute income in the interests of achieving greater equity and distributive justice. The social welfare and other measures designed to foster this objective can, and do, make allowance for the redistributive effects of price inflation and unemployment. Indeed, the Canada Pension Plan explicitly links benefits to changes in the cost of living. Along this line it might be argued that the primary task of stabilization policy is to maximize real output, and that those concerned with stabiliza-tion policy should leave it to other branches of the government already active in the field to achieve the distribution of income that is regarded as acceptable.

All of these questions are further complicated by the influence of external price changes on Canada's price level. It seems evident that Canadian employment and price-level objectives can be sensibly defined only in relation to the external factors conditioning Canadian wages, prices, unemployment, and the ability and willing-ness of governments to contain or offset these external influences. The scope for public action to offset external price changes is closely circumscribed if one assumes a fixed exchange rate and also that no Canadian government can allow the unemployment rate to rise and to fluctuate by the extent which might be necessary. In this connection, it is interesting to note that since 1920, with the excep-tion of the postwar period, interregional variations in changes in consumer prices in the United States have exceeded the differences in consumer price changes between it and Canada.[7] At the same time, it is questionable whether Canadian governments can simply back off and fully accept whatever external pressure is exerted on domestic prices without resisting such increases to some extent through aggregate demand policies.

The difficulties which external pressures create are illustrated in figures 3, 4, and 5, which have been calculated from our price-change–unemployment relationship.[8] Figure 3 indicates the unem-

[7]*Ibid.,* 190–2.

[8]All of these estimates assume that unit profits remain at their mean level from 1953 to 1965.

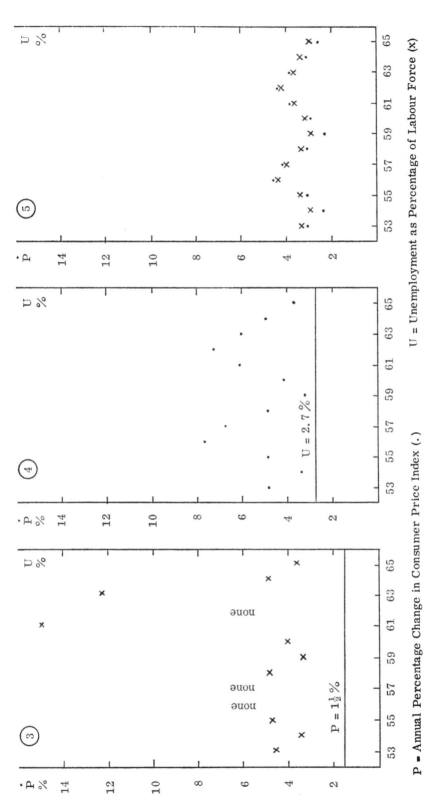

P = Annual Percentage Change in Consumer Price Index (.)   U = Unemployment as Percentage of Labour Force (x)

FIGS. 3, 4, and 5. Illustrative estimates of the rate of unemployment associated with various definitions of a general price objective, 1953–65.

ployment levels which would have been "required" in Canada to
restrict the rate of price increase consistently to 1½ per cent from
1953 to 1965, abstracting from lags and assuming the increases in
import prices and US wages which actually occurred. Figure 4
represents the opposite extreme. In this case the full effect of the
changes in import prices and US wages is absorbed into domestic
prices; unemployment is geared to the objective of restricting the
domestic component of the increase in prices to an increase of 1½
per cent per year. Figure 5 assumes that employment is regulated
with the objective of offsetting half of the influence of import prices
and US wages on Canadian prices and restricting the *domestic*
component of the increase in prices to 1½ per cent.

From figure 3 it is evident that any attempt to offset completely
the influence of external prices and wages not only would result in
highly volatile and frequently very high unemployment levels, but
also would frequently be impossible at any level of unemployment
that would be at all tolerable. Figure 4 suggests that a policy at the
other extreme would be equally intolerable in terms of the volatility
and the rate of increase in prices that would be implied. The middle
course depicted in figure 5 seems much more feasible, but even in
this case prices rise at an average annual rate of almost 3½ per
cent—an average rate which some people probably would regard
as intolerable and which could be reduced significantly only by
maintaining an average unemployment rate well in excess of 4
per cent per year. In short, if prices are generally increasing in the
world around us at rates comparable to those during the past
decade, any attempts to offset a substantial portion of the external
effect on domestic prices by repressing domestic demand may not
only prove very difficult to accomplish, but also may prove very
costly in terms of real income foregone if, in fact, the attempt is
successful.

By the same token, it is evident that Canada cannot realistically
aim at a long-run unemployment–price-change combination which
gives substantially greater priority to employment and less to price
stability than the unemployment–price-change combination at which
US policy aims. Attempting to do so would result in balance-of-payments difficulties, especially if the country remains on a fixed
exchange rate. Too much, however, can be made of this balance-of-
payments constraint. For one thing, there frequently is confusion

between the *current account* balance and the *balance-of-payments* position. During 1966, for instance, Canada has had a very strong balance-of-payments position, so strong in fact that the authorities elected to repatriate some $140 million of US-held Canadian government bonds in order to avoid further reserve accumulations. At the same time Canada was running a large deficit on current account. The constraint on Canada's freedom to pursue its own policy combination arises from the over-all balance-of-payments position, not from the current account balance.

It should also be recognized that the policy combination we are considering involves the consumer price index—not wholesale price or prices of internationally traded goods—and that there is no close and direct relationship between changes in the consumer price index and Canada's balance-of-payments position. Although there is an interrelation between price changes in various sectors of the economy, it is evident that the consumer price index is not simply a mirror image of wholesale or foreign prices. From 1953 to 1966, the consumer price index increased by about 25 per cent, the wholesale price index by 17 per cent, and the export price index by 16 per cent; the import price index increased by 21 per cent. One reason for this disparity between consumer price changes and wholesale and export price changes is that about 45 per cent of the consumer price index reflects the cost of housing and services which are not traded internationally. Increases in service costs since 1953 have averaged over 58 per cent, exceeding the increases in any other major components of the index by a considerable margin.

In addition, some freedom is afforded to Canadian policy in the choice of its price-change–unemployment objective by the possibility of adjusting the exchange rate and by the ease with which Canada in the past has been able to attract foreign capital.

In sum, it is indisputable that balance-of-payments considerations and a desire to avoid exchange rate changes substantially restrict Canada's freedom of choice in selecting an appropriate combination of price change and unemployment as the goal of stabilization policy. It bears equal emphasis, however, that this constraint does not eliminate all choice and that the country has some limited scope for selecting its stabilization objectives.

The main policy conclusions which emerge from this brief review may be summarized as follows:

(1) We should not assume that the difficulties facing economic policy in this country are more difficult than they really are by starting out from the premise that there is an inverse relationship between the long-run rate of economic growth and the level of employment. As far as one can tell, the secular growth rate is independent of the level of employment, and there may be a weak positive association. This implies that stabilization policies should be closely geared to the objectives of high employment and price stability.

(2) There can be little question that there is a conflict between the objectives of high employment and price stability. Policies that will reduce this conflict as much as possible, consistent with the other goals of our society, should be pursued. Even if this is done, there is little reason for believing that this conflict can be reduced to the point where it is no longer important.

(3) It is difficult to say with any assurance what is the optimum combination of unemployment and price change at which stabilization policy should aim. This issue poses important political and sociological, as well as economic, questions which in the final analysis are necessarily resolved by our political leaders. Nevertheless, if one looks only at economic considerations, one can argue that sometimes in the past there may have been some tendency to overestimate the costs of rising prices in relation to the costs of unemployment, and that the community as a whole would have had a higher real income if economic policy in this country had given higher priority to maintaining high employment and lower priority to restraining price increases.

(4) The relationship between the level of employment and the degree of price stability in this country is greatly influenced by external factors conditioning Canadian wages, prices, and unemployment. It seems wholly unrealistic to define either a price objective or an unemployment objective for this country without fully taking these external influences into account. Moreover, balance-of-payments considerations and a desire to avoid exchange rate movements seriously circumscribe the options open to Canadian policy. This constraint, however, does not completely eliminate all choice between the objectives of high employment and stable prices.

Reconciling Canada's Economic Goals

D. L. McQUEEN

In modern times, our economic goals tend to be more demanding, partly because we have more of them. The *First Annual Review* of the Economic Council of Canada sets out five major goals for the Canadian economy, and these may be taken as generally representative of the aspirations of most industrial countries. But in addition to having more goals, we set them higher than in the past and articulate them more precisely. In many cases we reduce them to simple and readily understandable statistics, and as a result substandard performance, whether it consists of slow growth, high unemployment, an excessive price rise, or some other unsatisfactory condition, is much more apparent to everyone and harder to explain away.

All this is not unreasonable. The performance standards which we set for national economies nowadays are more varied and severe than they used to be, but the policy tools available for meeting those standards are more numerous and powerful. Moreover, policies in support of one goal may in some instances promote the achievement of others. In a slack economy, for example, policies to restore full employment may also do a great deal to bring about faster economic growth. We must face the fact, though, that having more economic goals, and more demanding ones, inevitably increases the possibility of conflict between them.

When the government asked the Economic Council in 1965 to conduct a broad examination of prices, costs, incomes, and productivity, it was decided that the conflict between price and employment goals should be central to the enquiry. The terms of reference suggested that the Government was anxious, among other things, to explore additional options to find means of making its policy choices somewhat easier and to raise levels of achievement across the whole spectrum of economic goals. More specifically, the Council considered the question of how to arrest future price rises under conditions of economic buoyancy such as Canada experienced in 1965 and 1966. Please understand that the Council did not decry, and I do not now decry, the very remarkable achievements of the Canadian economy over the period of expansion which began in early 1961; there has been much in these achievements to cause rejoicing. But it has been plainly evident, especially in the last year or so, that the conflict between high employment and price stability still exists. For example, in 1965, when unemployment averaged 3.9 per cent of the labour force, the consumer price index averaged 2.4 per cent higher than in the previous year, but in 1966, with unemployment averaging 3.6 per cent of the labour force, the year-to-year increase in the consumer price index was 3.7 per cent. I shall confine myself to trying to explain how the problem of goal conflict, and the consequent need for doing more to reconcile Canada's economic goals, arises in the first place.

The state of our knowledge about the exact process by which the rate of price rise accelerates as the economy expands towards full employment is still badly deficient. This is particularly true in Canada, where there has been surprisingly little detailed research into the matter. We do, however, know enough to be able to say that ultra-simple "villain theories" of who is responsible for price increases by and large are not valid.

Once the rise in the general level of prices has become sufficiently rapid to attract widespread public concern, claims that the whole business is largely the work of a relatively small, easily identifiable group of malefactors should be regarded with scepticism. It is often suggested, for example, that the exercise of market power by large trade unions is obviously one of the major cases of upward pressure on wages and through wages on prices. This thesis understandably gains in popularity whenever there is brisk activity and disturbance on the collective-bargaining front, but it leaves some large questions unanswered. While union membership in Canada has made a notable leap forward in the last couple of years, it still appears to account for only about a third of the non-agricultural labour force. Yet even without unions to bargain for them, some elements at least of the unorganized two-thirds seem to have done reasonably well for themselves. If we look, for example, at salaries and wages in manufacturing over the period from 1949 to 1965, we find that average weekly salaries appear to have increased a trifle more than average weekly wages, i.e., 119 per cent compared with 110 per cent. We may observe, too, that over the same period there were some pronounced variations between industries, variations that cannot readily be explained by differences in the degree of union organization. Thus, average wages and salaries combined rose by fully 149 per cent in the construction industry, compared with 114 per cent in manufacturing; yet the percentages of union member-ship in the two industries were little different. Finally, I would mention that some of our staff studies have found that the basic wage gains obtained by unions in collective bargaining display a remarkable sensitivity to the general slackness or tightness of the economy. The power that is being exercised is at best a distinctly qualified power.

Another quite popular explanation of inflation puts the chief blame on a small group of large corporations, whose market power permits them to boost prices with impunity, and whose strategic position in the economy spreads the repercussions of their actions widely. Now this borders on a very real and important group of economic issues relating to the organization of industry and its many-faceted impact on economic behaviour. But the use of cor-porate market power (or, if you like, administered pricing) as a simple theory of inflation also leaves some major questions un-answered. If this power largely explains increases in the general price level, why is it that some of the earliest and most rapid increases in prices during a typical economic expansion occur in highly competitive markets, e.g., in markets for certain internation-ally traded primary commodities? And why does the rate of increase in the general price level, like union wage gains, display a strong if lagged relationship to the buoyancy or sluggishness of the whole economy?

In thus throwing cold water on the simpler types of villain theory,

I am not trying to persuade you that we are all of us—unions, corporations, public servants, or whoever—a band of innocents, gripped by mighty, impersonal forces which none of us ever does anything to influence in his own interest. There would be no virtue in trading one oversimplification for another, to the effect that it is all just a matter of "good-old-supply-and-demand." That would leave a lot of questions unanswered too, for example: Why is it that rises in many industrial prices are often not at all obviously related to waves of demand pressure for the particular goods and services involved?

Despite its shortcomings, good-old-supply-and-demand still can be very helpful. In making sense out of a situation of very strong, generalized inflationary pressure on the economy—a wartime or early postwar situation, for example—it can take us a long way. But we are not really talking about that kind of situation. We are talking about an economy with a serious conflict of goals: an economy which is getting too much price rise even while it is still a considerable distance below some widely accepted figure of full employment. We are also talking about an economy which is neither a model of perfect competition, nor yet the plaything of the totally planned corporation that Professor Galbraith now seems to be depicting for us, but which is, rather, strung out along a lengthy scale of varying degrees of imperfect competition.

To explain this kind of economy we need a mixed theory. We need a theory with plenty of good-old-supply-and-demand (more and more of it, indeed, as full employment is approached), but one which also takes realistic account of the actual pattern of industry and institutions, of the varying amounts of discretionary power that can be exercised over many prices, wages, and other rates of return, and of the climate of uncertainty and fluctuating expectations in which all these things work themselves out.

As of now, we have no such theory. We may have taken an important step towards one when Otto Eckstein published his article, "A Theory of the Wage-Price Process in Modern Industry,"[1] but there are still major gaps to be filled. For one thing, Eckstein was forced to limit himself to the manufacturing sector of the US

[1]Otto Eckstein, "A Theory of the Wage-Price Process in Modern Industry," *Review of Economic Studies*, October 1964.

economy because that is where the data are best and where most
of the relevant research has consequently been done. But manufacturing only accounts for about a third of both the US and
Canadian economies, and some of the most significant price-cost
developments of the recent period have occurred in other sectors,
such as services and construction.

Lacking a comprehensive and well-tested theory, we have to
theorize, to put together some sort of interim explanation that
roughly fits at least a fair proportion of the visible facts. Fortunately, many of these facts repeat themselves in recognizable
patterns and cycles. Many of us past the first blush of youth must
have had a strong feeling last summer, when price and wage
developments were much in the headlines and certain familiar
arguments and rebuttals began to be heard, that we had been here
before. And of course we had, notably in 1956–57, although as I
shall mention there have been one or two interesting differences
this time around.

What it comes down to is that in Canada, to a greater extent
than in most overseas countries, worrisome rises in the general price
level and serious conflicts between the goals of high employment
and price stability have thus far been a sometime thing, a phenomenon of the short-term business cycle. They have tended to force
themselves on our attention in the middle-to-late phases of strong
business-cycle expansions in the economy and to hold the stage for
a while after the peaks of expansion have been passed. At other
times, covering a quite substantial proportion of the postwar period,
they have not on the whole been one of our major economic
problems. This, of course, largely reflects the fact that many of
these other times have been times of considerable softness in the
economy.

Let us begin our attempted explanation at the low point of the
business cycle, at the outset of a new economic expansion. Let us
make one very important assumption: the broad instruments of
fiscal and monetary policy, acting on total demand, will be so
operated as to allow the economy to rise—not abruptly, but reasonably smoothly and steadily—towards full employment and full
potential output.

Now, while we can usefully talk about a steady expansion of the economy as a whole, we must keep in mind that at the level of individual industries and products things are rarely that easy. Some demands increase much faster than others, and the pattern of demand is constantly shifting. Automobiles and other consumer durables may be a leading sector of demand growth for a while, then demand for machinery and other investment goods may come on strongly and take over the lead. Manpower and other productive resources must not merely increase in order to meet these demands, they must also be transferred about the economy, especially when the pattern of demand growth undergoes major shifts.

A general economic expansion is in reality a most complex process, and it is not surprising that hitches and bottlenecks develop. The economy does not move up to its full potential all of a piece. Some parts of it hit short-term ceilings much sooner than others. Shortages of particular kinds of labour, raw materials, and other productive resources come to light, leading to some price rises and above-average wage increases. In the early stages of expansion, however, these are unlikely to be very numerous or to spread very far. This is partly because the continuing slack in the economy tends to limit the duration of shortages and to discourage the pushing up of cost increases into final prices. But the general state of psychology is also important. After a recession, and especially after a relatively prolonged experience of slow growth and weak demand such as we had in Canada in the late fifties and early sixties, people tend to run scared. Even the possessors of relatively substantial market power are usually disinclined, for the time being, to push their luck very far. They wonder if the new expansion of the economy is real and durable. Though not as exposed to it as some others, they worry about competition—domestic and foreign, actual and potential. Price rises at this stage might turn some big buyers to other sources or even to entering the business themselves. Union thinking, too, is apt to be cautious and recession-oriented at this stage, with more than usual stress on job and union-security objectives as compared with wage gains.

As the economy goes on expanding, however, these various restraining influences lose some of their power; with less total slack in the economy, bottlenecks become more numerous and longer-lived. Output catches up with existing plant capacity in more and more industries, and the pattern of demand growth shifts strongly towards investment in new productive facilities. In Canada, with its exceptionally high ratio of capital to output and its volatile pattern of investment spending, this is a very crucial phase of expansion. It imposes particular strains on the non-residential construction industry, which is characteristically called upon to expand its skilled labour force and other productive resources much faster than most other industries. Indeed, in 1963–65 the industry moved all the way from depressed to boom conditions in little more than two years. With such a burden of adjustment, it is small wonder that the construction sector periodically becomes an important centre of shortages, bottlenecks, and strong wage and price pressures that tend to exert an influence on other parts of the economy. This is all the more so because one of the great safety valves of the Canadian economy—the relief of domestic pressures by importing from abroad—cannot be fully operative in the case of construction. Materials, manpower, and managerial know-how can be imported to some degree, but not, by and large, the completed product.

Once it becomes clear that the economy has a boom on its hands (and this almost inevitably means that the American economy, too, is enjoying considerable prosperity), psychology tends to adjust, and indeed to over-adjust. People run less scared. Economic risk-taking of all kinds becomes popular again, together with the taking of a keen interest in the gains that others are making. Price increases and unusually large wage increases occur in some sectors and have at least a degree of repercussion elsewhere. Union negotiators, for example, come under stronger pressure from their memberships to obtain favourable settlements. If the cost of living has started to rise appreciably, this will add to the pressure. Businessmen, for their part, are more inclined to give ground on wages and salaries, partly because profits are improved and the labour market is tighter, but partly too, in some cases, because a more relaxed reading of the competitive situation gives the impression that cost increases can with less danger be passed into price increases. This may not always take place immediately; it may await a later phase of the business cycle, when, typically, productivity gains have declined and profit margins per unit of output have come under more of a squeeze.

Few if any of the participants in the process really believe that boom conditions will last forever; indeed, in the North American environment this is one of the basic difficulties. Experience of economic fluctuations brings about a feeling of now or never, a disposition to make hay while the sun shines. When the sun does finally cloud over and the economy loses its expansive momentum, considerable upward movement of prices typically persists for a while. This largely reflects various lags in the system, some fairly mechanical, others more psychological in nature. It is important to recognize this delayed-action development for what it is and not to take policy measures based on the assumption that the economy is still expanding vigorously.

To recapitulate a little, serious conflict between the objectives of high employment and reasonable price stability in Canada has tended to reveal itself at certain stages of the short-term business cycle. It has been closely associated with the time lags and other recurrent patterns of the business cycle, for example, the relative movement of wages and profits. The most rapid increases in profits generally occur early in the expansion, at which stage profits gain relatively to wages. Later, however, the relative gains are reversed, and profits tend to be squeezed. This fluctuation over time means that by picking dates carefully, almost anything about wages and profits can be proved, and of course this is one of the games that people play, some proving that profits are too high relative to wages, some that they are too low. Too often overlooked is the fact that in the longer run, these short-term oscillations cancel out to a large extent, and the wage-profit relationship exhibits a considerable degree of stability.

In the course of a typical business-cycle expansion, the rate of general price rise tends to accelerate, through a process which cannot readily be characterized as either cost-push or demand-pull, but which contains elements of both. The ultimate movement of final prices usually has many apparent earmarks of cost-push, and the majority of those who raise prices probably believe themselves to be victims of cost-push. But a tracing back of the process into the markets for labour, raw materials, and other factors of production, together with a careful consideration of the pervasive influence of general buoyancy in the economy, will usually result in greater weight being given to demand factors than at first seemed likely.

This has been a brief and outrageously selective sketch of a very complex process. Let me, through the medium of a sort of question-and-answer monologue, at least mention some further, highly important aspects.

First, what about money? Surely money matters. Surely it is at the heart of any inflationary process.

To a very large extent, I would agree. Money, and its management by the central bank, matter a great deal. Almost any conceivable kind of continued rise in the general price level, whether it is cost-push, demand-pull, creeping, walking, or running inflation, requires for its validation and sustenance an increasing money supply. But so does the desirable physical expansion of the economy, up to its rising path of full potential output. The monetary authorities, too, must have regard, not merely to one, but to several important economic goals. By managing monetary expansion with astuteness and forethought and by avoiding sharp discontinuities as far as possible, they can guard us against really severe inflation and may be able to contribute something towards diminishing the goal-conflict with which we are here concerned. But even a superlative performance by the central bank and by the fiscal authorities would seem likely to leave a substantial residual problem, calling for additional policy approaches.

Second, what about Canada's open economy and the great world outside?

This, of course, matters very much also, in two principal ways. Canada's dependence on foreign trade makes the goal of reasonable price stability all the more important from the standpoint of international competitiveness. But the openness of the economy also means that it is unusually subject to forces rolling in from outside and profoundly affecting the behaviour of prices and costs, as well as many other aspects of Canadian economic performance. Needless to say, a great many of these forces (they are not all unfavourable forces, by any means) roll in from the United States. It was convenient not to mention a moment ago that much of the process of price rise during cyclical expansions that I was trying to describe is really more a North American than a Canadian phenomenon, but it should be mentioned now. This is something we have to live with. It means that we cannot be rigid about our price-stability objectives, but must conceive them flexibly, with a sharp and realistic eye on the course of developments in the United States and elsewhere. We are not exempt, however, from some very substantial home-grown sources of potential price and cost pressures, notably in our service and investment goods sectors. It will be important to see if we cannot devise better and more efficient means of containing these pressures during periods of expansion.

The rate of growth of productivity—of physical output per person employed—is a third aspect deserving special mention. Productivity growth is important in the short run, where fluctuations in it are an integral part of the business cycle. It is also important in the longer run, where it appears to operate in Canada as a persistent dampening influence on the rate of price increase—this, of course, in addition to its contribution to the growth of the economy's total real output. Policies tending directly or indirectly to stimulate productivity are bound to form a large part of any package of workable measures for achieving better reconciliation of Canada's economic goals.

A word of caution is in order, however. From the standpoint of diagnosis, the mathematical relationships between productivity and incomes, costs, and prices are almost too simple—deceptively so. They are not the key to everything that they sometimes appear. For instance, people are continually discovering that wages sometimes increase faster than productivity, that this implies a rise in unit labour cost, and that this in turn is frequently accompanied by a rise in the price level. They feel that they hold in their hand the very essence of the inflationary process. But this is not necessarily the case. There are many varieties of inflationary process, and nearly every one of them if sustained for any length of time will sooner or later be featured by a rise in unit labour cost. But is this mostly symptom or cause? This is the beginning, not the end, of the diagnosis.

Finally, let me return to the subject of market power as it relates to the reconciliation of high employment and price stability. I suggested earlier that while simple villain theories of inflation were not airworthy, there must nevertheless be a place for market power in our thinking about the kind of mixed process of moderate or partial inflation that gives rise to the problem under discussion.

I wish that it were possible to give you more solid information about the consistency and proportions of the particular Canadian mixture. Our research in this regard did not progress as fast as we hoped it would. Work continues, however, and on the corporate side the Council's new reference from the Government in the area of consumer interests, mergers, monopolies, patents, etc., will entail looking at market power in a broader economic context.

On the union side, one new point seems to emerge from recent Canadian experience. The wage outcome of collective bargaining, as we sometimes tend to forget, is the proximate result not merely of union push, but of union push and employer resistance. The strength of employer resistance varies over time and is much affected by the state of the market for the employer's product—its buoyancy, its competitiveness. For this reason, more sophisticated worriers about connections between collective bargaining and rising prices tend to concentrate their attention on industries where substantial union bargaining power in the labour market co-exists with substantial employer power in the product market.

But a significant and rapidly growing proportion of recent collective bargaining in Canada has been with another kind of employer, one with an unusual product market and generally no profit margin. I refer to the government or public sector of the economy, broadly defined. We have recently seen in this sector a remarkable breakthrough of new union organization, a number of large settlements (some undoubtedly including elements of "catch-up" to comparable remuneration elsewhere), and a general disturbance of the collective-bargaining atmosphere, which appears to have had at least some effect on wage determination in other parts of the economy. To some extent we face here a new situation for which we have still to work out fully appropriate ground rules and procedures.

This has been an attempt to explain how conflict between the objectives of high employment and reasonable price stability typically arises in Canada. It has been based partly on theorizing and on what is known in the trade as "casual empiricism," but also in part on the more respectable foundation of the economic literature of business cycles. The problem of reconciling these two important Canadian economic goals is tough and complex. It will not disappear overnight, and it is unlikely by nature to yield to any simple, sweeping solution based on a diagnosis of the same character. Much remains to be learned about it, but enough is known to warrant trying out a number of different lines of attack. It looks very much like the sort of problem that has to be worked on from various angles, with patience and an attitude that any substantial progress will be worthwhile. The main thing is to begin.

FOREIGN EXPERIENCE

Foreign Experience with Incomes Policies

ARTHUR M. ROSS

Incomes policies are one aspect of an increasingly active government intervention in modern economies. In all advanced industrial societies there is a strong commitment to full employment and economic growth. The attendant problem of cost-push inflation, at or near full employment, leads to political unrest, economic maladjustments, and balance-of-payment difficulties. The authorities are then required to "cool off" the economy, causing unemployment and additional unrest.

Experiments with incomes policy, thus far largely inconclusive, attempt to eliminate the need to choose between excessive unemployment and excessive price increases. While the degree of concern over inflation varies from one country to another, it is not true that any nation can assume permanent responsibility for the employment level and remain persistently indifferent to costs and prices.

Not only have many countries experimented with incomes policies, but many formats have been used. There have been four principal versions. The first is a general formula relating productivity, wage increases, costs, and prices, with major reliance on persuasion. The wage-price guideposts in the United States are the most prominent example. Second, incomes policy may be one element in a system of national economic planning or indicative programming, as in France. Third, there may be special bipartisan or tripartite bodies charged with the task of implementing official wage and price policies. Examples include the Foundation of Labour in Holland and the former National Economic Development Council in the United Kingdom. Often the objective of preserving industrial peace is interwoven with that of attaining price stability. Finally, incomes policy may take the form of temporary wage-price "stops," "pauses," or "freezes" in balance-of-payments emergencies. Among the nations which have resorted to this device are Great Britain in 1961 and 1966, Denmark in 1963, and Australia in 1962.

The essential purpose of wage and price restraints is to minimize increases in unit labour costs and price levels. Yet it is very difficult to find any perceptible correlation between the existence of formal wage-price or incomes policies, on the one hand, and the degree of cost and price stability on the other. Neither does the existence of special bipartite or tripartite machinery appear to affect the results in any systematic way. Emergency actions of a mandatory character, such as the price freeze in France in recent years, do show up in the statistics. But it does not seem possible to isolate the effect of informal controls of the guidepost variety. For example, two of the European countries with the most elaborate organization for incomes policy have been the Netherlands and the United Kingdom, and they have the highest labour cost indexes (on a 1953 base), with the exception of France, and are in the upper half of countries in terms of consumer price indexes.

Italy, Germany, and Japan were the countries with the most stable labour costs and the most stable wholesale prices in the period up to 1960. Incomes policy was not emphasized in any of these countries prior to 1960, although German governments have made some ineffective pronouncements in more recent years.

The difficulty of interpreting the statistics does not prove that incomes policies have been insignificant. An alternative explanation would be that the impact has been overshadowed and outweighed by other influences on costs and prices. Among these other influences are differences in unemployment rates. The United States, for example, has had the best record from the standpoint of holding prices down, but at the same time has had higher unemployment than most other countries. There have also been differences in productivity growth. Italy, Germany, and Japan, their industries having been levelled during the Second World War, undertook the task of reconstruction in the postwar period and had unusually high rates of productivity growth until recently. This made it possible to support high rates of wage increases, also beginning from a low level, without the concomitant inflation. In addition, there have been differences in labour-force growth. Here again Germany had an advantage in being able to make use of refugees from Eastern Europe, as well as imported workers from Italy, Spain, and Greece. Thus the evidence is too interwoven to say exactly what the impact has been, but it is doubtless significant that in a real squeeze countries tend to resort to temporary wage-price freezes.

The current policy in Great Britain will serve as an example. It was developed from a joint statement of intent of December 1964 signed by the Government, the Trades Union Congress, and employers' organizations. Steps were taken to construct a voluntary "early-warning" system, but it was clear by July 1966 that incomes were expanding out of proportion to the actual rise in productivity. As part of the drastic measures considered necessary to deal with pressures on sterling, the Government called for a voluntary "stand-still" of prices and incomes until the end of the year, followed by a period of severe restraint during the first half of 1967. At the same time the Government sought, and obtained, the power to make these policies mandatory in the Prices and Incomes Act of 1966 and decided to bring its reserve powers into operation on October 6 of that year. Under these powers, the period from July to the end of December was treated as one of absolute wage freeze, and the first half of 1967 was a period of "severe restraint" designed to minimize wage increases within the framework of the prices and incomes policy according to principles laid down in a white paper of November 1966. While the reaction of management and unions has by no means been enthusiastic, the policies adopted by the Government have been generally complied with.

One of the most difficult problems of the incomes policy in the United Kingdom and Europe has been that of wage drift. This may be defined as a tendency for actual worker earnings to become disassociated from the ostensible wage rates set forth in collective-bargaining contracts or other schedules. Wage drift occurs when the established wage rates become unrealistic because of demand pressures in a tight labour market. There have been numerous forms of wage drift, including job evaluation plans installed unilaterally by employers or developed in agreement with works councils, loose incentive rates, systematic overtime, sometimes at least partly spurious, and local agreements between shop-steward councils and plant management. Under these circumstances, the industry-wide or regional collective-bargaining agreements, which are characteristic of European systems, have often produced unrealistic results far below the wages actually paid and received; nominal compliance with incomes policy criteria has often been of little significance. Wage drift has not been a problem in the United States, where rates of pay and fringe benefits are negotiated on a local basis, more often than not, and are therefore not likely to become dissociated from labour-market pressures.

Another difficult problem in the United Kingdom and Europe has been the apparent inequity suffered by workers in the public sector. It is always easier for a government to regulate the wages of its own employees—those in enterprises closely controlled by the government—than of those in the private sector generally. Therefore teachers, civil servants, employees of government-owned transportation systems, etc., have often felt the brunt of incomes policies in practice. A great many of the recent strikes in France have been short demonstration stoppages by public-sector employees in protest against what they regarded as illiberal wage policies.

I turn now to a more detailed discussion of wage and price guideposts in the United States. The economic controls adopted during the two world wars and the Korean conflict must be regarded as part of wartime mobilization programmes and are therefore beyond the scope of this paper. The modern wage-price guideposts had their beginning in statements by President Truman's Council of Economic Advisers in 1952, to the effect that the rise in wages should be kept in line with the improvement of productivity, estimated at that time as between 2 and 3 per cent per year. President Eisenhower's Council of Economic Advisers offered some rather vague and general advice to the same effect on more than one occasion. At the same time, a theory of cost-push inflation, heavily influenced by the circumstances of the capital boom in the late fifties, was emerging in the writings of Charles Schultze, Otto Eckstein, and others.

The wage-price guideposts were given for specific and pointed application by the Council of Economic Advisers in its famous Economic Report of 1962. The original formulation in the report was:

> The general guide for noninflationary wage behavior is that the rate of increase in wage rates (including fringe benefits) in each industry be equal to the trend rate of overall productivity increase. General acceptance of this guide would maintain stability of labor cost per unit of output for the economy as a whole—though not of course for individual industries. . . .
>
> The general guide for noninflationary price behavior calls for price reduction if the industry's rate of productivity increase exceeds the overall rate—for this would mean declining unit labor costs; it calls for an appropriate increase in price if the opposite situation prevails; and it calls for stable prices if the two rates of productivity increase are equal.[1]

These were advanced as "general guideposts." The Council recognized that "to reconcile them with objectives of equity and efficiency, specific modifications must be made to adapt them to the circumstances of particular industries." The most important exceptions cited in 1962 were:

> (1) Wage rate increases would exceed the general guide rate in an industry which would otherwise be unable to attract sufficient labor; or in which wage rates are exceptionally low compared with the range of wages earned elsewhere by similar labor, because the bargaining position of workers has been weak in particular local labor markets.
>
> (2) Wage rate increases would fall short of the general guide rate in an industry which could not provide jobs for its entire labor force even in times of generally full employment; or in which wage rates are exceptionally high compared with the range of wages earned elsewhere by similar labor, because the bargaining position of workers has been especially strong.
>
> (3) Prices would rise more rapidly, or fall more slowly, than indicated by the general guide rate in an industry in which the level of profits was insufficient to attract the capital required to finance a needed expansion in capacity; or in which costs other than labor costs had risen.

[1]*Economic Report of the President*, together with the *Annual Report of the Council of Economic Advisers* (Washington, D.C.: US Government Printing Office, 1963), 189.

(4) Prices would rise more slowly, or fall more rapidly, than indicated by the general guide in an industry in which the relation of productive capacity to full employment demand shows the desirability of an outflow of capital from the industry; or in which costs other than labor costs have fallen; or in which excessive market power has resulted in rates of profit substantially higher than those earned elsewhere on investments of comparable risk (p. 189).

The Council made it plain that wage and price guideposts were not intended to be a substitute for vigorous fiscal and monetary policies. The belief was, however, that they could supplement the results for these more traditional measures and permit employment to be stimulated more than would otherwise be possible.

Problems of interpretation arose with the publication of these more precise standards. First, were they intended to be educational, or were they subject to enforcement by the Administration? Second, how were the standards to be applied? Was a wage increase of 3 to 3½ per cent to be viewed as a limit, or were the guideposts to be used as a policy tool in a few key situations such as basic steel, or were the various rules and exceptions to be taken seriously? In the latter case, how were the "exceptions" to be interpreted? Who was to decide when wages of a particular industry were "exceptionally high," when labour's bargaining position was "weak" or "exceptionally strong," when an industry had "sufficient" or "insufficient" capital, and so on?

The first year's experience was somewhat equivocal. The steel wage settlement was praised for being non-inflationary, and the Administration staved off what would have been a damaging increase in steel prices. The wage settlement for non-operating railroad employees won a presidential blessing, but if the guideposts had been taken seriously the increase would have been smaller, considering the rapidly declining employment trend in the industry. In any event it is doubtful that the increase would have been any larger in the absence of the guideposts. In the shipping and airline industries, wage settlements far out of line with the guideposts were developed with the assistance of federal mediators, emergency boards, and special representatives. In the construction industry large annual increases were negotiated in contracts running from three to five years in duration.

In 1963, as in 1962, the principal guidepost incidents involved the steel industry. In April the major producers made some selective price increases amounting to a one per cent advance in the industry's price level. President Kennedy commented that they had "acted with some restraint," and expressed the hope that other companies—"particularly in the oil industry," as well as the Steelworkers' Union—would do likewise. In June the Steelworkers accepted a new contract, to run from July 30, 1963, to May 31, 1965. There was no wage increase, and the fringe benefits did not amount to more than 3 per cent per year.

Under the circumstances of 1962–63, with the unemployment rate hovering close to 6 per cent, it is doubtful that inflation was such a serious threat as to justify active emphasis on wage and price restraint. At the beginning of 1964, however, it seemed apparent that the income-tax cut would soon be enacted. The Council endeavoured to tighten up the exceptions to the guideposts lest they become the general rule: "The general guideposts can cover the vast majority of wage and price decisions. . . . The modifications of the guideposts still apply, but it must be emphasized that they are intended to apply to only a relatively few cases."

In addition, the 1964 report included the well-known 3.2 per cent, described as the "average annual percentage change in output per man-hour during the latest 5 years." This immediately became the *de facto* standard of wage increases, and the exceptions faded into the background. Likewise, the language concerning price cuts became part of the background music.

The important applications of the price guideposts in 1964–66 (at least those which have been the subject of public discussion) have been mainly in basic raw materials industries: steel, aluminum, and copper. In the latter two cases, government-owned stockpiles were available to stabilize the market. The principal wage cases have been the 1964 auto contracts, the 1965 steel agreement, and the Federal Civil Service Employees' Pay Act of 1965. The annual cost of the auto settlement, including fringe benefits, was something over 4 per cent; President Johnson expressed the hope that "other industries with profits below the high levels in the automobile industry will not use the auto settlement as a pattern." The steel settlement was consistent with the guideposts when all the complications of timing were taken into account, while the federal employees' Pay Act provided an average increase of 3.6 per cent.

In its 1966 report the Council decided to drop the five-year moving average of productivity changes in the private economy:

Now that the economy is at the end of its fifth year of uninterrupted expansion, a five-year moving average no longer gives a reasonable approximation of the true productivity trend. The last recession year (1960) drops out of the average; yet the unsustainable productivity gains of a year of recovery (1961) and four years of improving utilization of productive capacity are retained. . . . It appears that the long-term trend, independent of cyclical swings, is slightly over 3 percent.[2]

On these grounds the Council recommended that the 3.2 per cent wage guideposts be continued.

As 1966 proceeded, resistance to government intervention and wage and price decisions increased within the ranks of labour and management. With the consumer price index increasing at a rate of over 3 per cent per year, it was manifestly unreasonable to expect that wage increases could be held to an average of 3.2 per cent. While some business firms withheld price increases or rolled them back at the request of the Administration, other attempts were less successful. By the end of the year, it was evident that the guideposts had run out of steam for the time being at least. In its 1967 report the Council wisely restricted itself to a reaffirmation of the general principles involved, without stating a specific percentage figure for wage increases.

As noted earlier, it is extremely difficult to evaluate the effect of wage-price guideposts in preserving economic stability, inasmuch as the record is beclouded by the mixture of many influences. Whether the guideposts held down prices and wages from 1962 to 1966 is a highly controversial question in the United States. It is clear that the rate of advance was less than in the fifties, while unemployment rates were comparable. Yet there are few leaders of either management or labour who will admit to having been influenced by guideposts when the time came to make actual decisions. My own opinion is that the guidepost emphasis was helpful in promoting

[2]*Economic Report of the President*, together with *The Annual Report of the Council of Economic Advisers* (Washington, D.C.: US Government Printing Office, 1966), 92.

wider understanding of the economic relationships involved and did affect the climate of negotiations, and that occasional pressures on major producers, such as those in the steel and aluminum industries, must have had a moderating influence on price increases.

In sum, the problem of cost-price inflation cannot be swept under the rug as long as a government is devoted to achieving and maintaining full employment. Emergency price and wage freezes will work for a while, but it is not clear that any country has devised a successful formula, which will work over a longer period of time, as an alternative to mandatory wage and price controls.

I believe that the guidepost issue will rise again in the United States, although not right away. Considerable time will probably elapse before the economic, political, and technical issues can be resolved, before the views of labour and management become more positive, and before the public is prepared for effective "second generation" wage-price policies. Such policies would not be based solely on the long-term trend of productivity, but would take cognizance of the aggregate division of national income, the level of profits, and other sensitive matters. They might also involve intimate collaboration between the government and the principal interest groups, although none of these parties is presently prepared and would doubtless label any such collaboration as economic planning, or statism, in today's economic and political environment.

Nevertheless, we ought to look ahead and assume, at least for the purpose of argument, that we will have a second generation of wage-price policies. What is likely to be the general formula relating productivity, wages, and prices if guideposts should be reconstructed in the future? How will this formula be applied to specific periods of time and to the circumstances of specific cases? And what procedures will be necessary to secure acceptance, involvement, and participation on the part of management, labour, and other interested groups?

In speaking of the general formulation (which I distinguish from particular application to a given year) we can begin by noting that a long-term productivity trend is not a wage policy. Many other matters must be taken into account, and these cannot be brushed aside as exceptions or deviations.

A timely example is a rise in the consumer price index, which was not allowed for in the original formulation by the Council of Economic Advisers. Consumer prices can rise for reasons having nothing at all to do with the market power of companies and unions: the unexpected impact of a war situation, agricultural harvest, raw material price fluctuations on the world market, etc. In addition, in a prosperous economy it must be taken for granted that prices of services—representing mainly income to workers in the service industries—will increase steadily, because higher incomes are not offset by corresponding increases in productivity.

Likewise, the long-term productivity trend cannot be the only factor affecting price decisions. Labour costs, profit levels, capital needs, the economic impact of higher prices, and many other factors must be taken into account. In attempting a general restatement of relationships among wages, productivity, and prices I would offer the following thoughts:

(1) For reasons stated above it is not practical to seek complete stability of the consumer price index.

(2) It is more important to have stable prices of industrial products at wholesale. These reflect basic trends in costs and efficiency and affect the American position in world markets.

(3) The consumer price index will run about one per cent ahead of the wholesale industrial price index.

(4) Inasmuch as wholesale industrial products merged mainly from manufacturing industries, the labour-cost objectives should be the stabilized unit labour costs (or achieve a substantial degree of stability) in manufacturing, rather than in the total economy or total private economy.

(5) The productivity trend in manufacturing runs about 0.6 per cent ahead of the total private economy in a typical year. If the productivity trend is 3.2 per cent in the private economy, it is about 3.8 per cent in manufacturing. If this were the general standard for money wage increases, then labour costs would tend to remain stable in manufacturing.

(6) Since we assume that the consumer price index will be rising, real wage rates will not increase as rapidly as money wage rates. It follows logically that the long-run trend of real wage rates for all wage and salary earners must be related not to the productivity trend in manufacturing (3.8 per cent, we are assuming) and

not to a trend in the total private economy (3.2 per cent), but to the trend for the total economy, including government.

Employees of local, state, and federal governments now make up 15 per cent of the labour force, and public sector personnel demand and receive compensation increases. Like the increases enjoyed by employees in the private sector these must be paid out of the productivity dividend. At the same time any increase in output per man-hour in the public sector contributes to the productivity dividend.

The problem is that there is no available measure of product or productivity in the public sector. Output is equated with man-hour input, automatically yielding a zero productivity trend as an accounting convention. I do not know when we will be able to measure product and productivity of government in terms which are applied to other activities, but we cannot go on assuming that the total-economy productivity trend is 3.2 per cent. If we continue to follow the established accounting convention, a zero trend in government, combined with a 3.2 per cent trend in the private sector, would yield a 2.8 per cent trend for the private economy. (If the productivity increase in government is 1 per cent a year, the total-economy trend rises to 2.9 per cent. If the trend is 2 per cent in government, it is 3.0 per cent in the total economy. But if the public sector were to be incorporated in a self-contained and consistent model, a price index for government services would have to be included in the consumer price index.)

Putting these factors together, second-generation guideposts might consist of the following:

A. Formula for price stability

(1) Productivity trend in manufacturing: 3.8 per cent.

(2) Money-wage guidepost: 3.8 per cent a year on the average.

(3) Consumer price index increase: 1.0 per cent.

(4) Real-wage increase: 2.8 per cent a year on the average.

(5) Productivity trend in total economy: 2.8 per cent (continuing to treat the public sector in the established way).

(6) Labour costs and prices of wholesale industrial products: level.

B. Formula for "substantial" price stability

(1) Productivity trend in manufacturing: 3.8 per cent.

(2) Money-wage guidepost: 4.3 per cent a year on the average.

(3) Consumer price index increase: 1.5 per cent.

(4) Real-wage increase: 2.8 per cent a year on the average.

(5) Productivity trend in total economy: 2.8 per cent (continuing to treat the public sector in the established way).

(6) Labour costs and prices of wholesale industrial products: increase of 0.5 per cent.

I have been speaking about the relationships between wages, prices, productivity, and profits in a wage-price restraint enterprise which might come to maturity in the 1970s. But although economic understanding is crucial, statistics and correlations do not constitute a policy or a programme. A viable programme will have other elements. The basic relationships will be translated into specific applications in the light of the particular circumstances of any given year. The principal interest groups such as industry, labour, and agriculture, and the most directly affected government agencies will be involved along with the Council of Economic Advisers. There will be periodic appraisals of price and wage developments in the light of the specific objectives which have been formulated for a particular period.

The first-generation guideposts are incomplete in that they are limited to an exposition of long-term relationships. They do not handle specific short-run problems which are certain to arise from time to time. It would not be practical to anticipate every contingency which might have an effect on a wage-price restraint programme. Therefore, an annual economic review will be essential for bringing together long-run objectives and short-run contingencies. Suppose that raw material prices have shot up through the ceiling on world markets? Suppose the government decides that every family should be assured an annual income of at least $3,000? Suppose a massive effort to rehabilitate urban slums is launched? Suppose that a medium-sized war breaks out? Suppose that payroll taxes are increased substantially in order to finance a corresponding increase in social-security benefits? Suppose that the wages of agricultural workers and low-paid service workers are substantially increased through an amendment to the minimum wage law? It would be impossible to ignore the impact of these developments on price and wage policy in the private sector.

Therefore, the terms of price and wage restraint should take the form of specific conclusions emerging from the annual economic review between the private-sector interest groups and the government authorities. The statement of conclusions should be the government's responsibility rather than a negotiated tripartite agreement. Similarly there should be a quarterly review of results, an appraisal of how they line up against the objectives for the year.

Some Issues
in the
Incomes Policy
Debate

DAVID C. SMITH

From a mysterious topic that few people were interested in discussing not too long ago incomes policy has recently emerged as a mysterious topic which many people in Canada are discussing. The air of mystery has undoubtedly been due in part to the difficulties of pinning down a clearly identifiable meaning for this type of policy. The range of other titles that have been used in place of it abroad—wage-price guideposts, guiding lights or guidelines for incomes and prices, an incomes and prices pause or freeze, national value programming—have often been like brand names that can indicate an important differentiation of a product, but they have also confused the foreign observer. In addition, there are some good things that can be said about an incomes policy and there are some bad things that can be said about it. As a result, the topic has the necessary ingredients to arouse curiosity, bewilderment, and controversy in public discussions.

In the following I shall try to pull together briefly[1] some of the issues in the incomes policy debate that foreign experiences have shown to be important and that should be considered in Canadian discussions of this type of policy. The approach will be a kind of cost-benefit analysis in which both the pros and cons have to be

[1]A fuller discussion of these issues is in David C. Smith, *Incomes Policies: Some Foreign Experiences and Their Relevance for Canada.* Special study no. 4, Economic Council of Canada (Ottawa: Queen's Printer, 1966).

weighed and in which the possibility of superior alternatives has to be considered. But first it is necessary to consider the meaning of an "incomes policy" for purposes of this paper.

Economic policy discussions in many Western countries have recently been dominated by the problem of achieving a greater control over general price movements while maintaining high employment levels. At least four broad lines of approach to tackling this problem can be noted in many countries. First, there has been the interest in exploring the costs and benefits of achieving a better performance on price stability if there are sacrifices in terms of other goals such as low unemployment. For example, there has been much discussion in the United Kingdom on the advantages of a slightly higher unemployment rate if this would mean greater price stability, fewer balance-of-payments difficulties, and a moderation of the stop-go policies that have been unsettling to growth. Second, much attention has been given to the question of improving on the past management of general demand conditions through monetary, fiscal, and exchange-rate policies in the hope that the extent of the conflicts among economic goals, observed in the past, can be reduced. Third, there has been a growing interest in many Western countries in policies influencing economic adjustment mechanisms and supply conditions. Measures that would improve the flexibility and adaptability of the economy, such as labour-market policies, improved commercial policies, and better competition policies, have all been recognized as relevant for reducing price stability problems at high employment levels. Finally, a number of Western countries have been experimenting with means of specifying directly what individual prices, wages, and, sometimes, other forms of money income should be. Incomes policy fits into this fourth category of approaches.

Very broadly, then, the distinctive feature of an incomes policy in relation to other economic policies is the attempt by governments to formulate and gain compliance to a set of criteria for money incomes and prices. The basic aim is to provide centralized objective standards on which to judge individual wage and price decisions and thereby to gain a more direct control over general price movements.

This approach is not, of course, new. For example, in the Middle

Ages the idea of a just price for products and labour was important
in Europe. Both the formulation of standards for a just price and
the expectation of compliance to these standards was closely linked
to the pervasive influence of religion on economic life. In wartime
many Western countries, including Canada, have resorted to cen-
trally determined standards for incomes and prices to control the
degree of inflation and to moderate profiteering from the war.
Public support for implementing the standards was greater in these
conditions because of the national cohesion from the war effort.

In recent years the surge of interest in incomes policy has been
based on the view that simple, but economically defensible, criteria
for incomes and prices, which would improve on the results of
market forces, could be formulated and that compliance to them
could be gained without detailed controls. Presumably a combination of three steps is required. The authorities have to formulate a
target for the desirable movement of the general price level. Next,
criteria for individual decisions affecting prices, wages, and, perhaps, other forms of income need to be specified. Then, there is the
problem of developing the devices that can be expected to encourage or compel compliance to the criteria.

Since considerable variation is possible in these three steps, it is
not surprising to find important differences in the forms incomes
policies have taken among countries and within countries over
time. The target for the average movement of money incomes was
linked in the case of the United States wage-price guideposts and
at times in British incomes policy to the trend in productivity. But
in four postwar periods in the United Kingdom there has been an
attempt to secure simply a short-run halt in the rise in money
wages. Over much of the postwar period in the Netherlands the
room for general wage and price increases was discussed in the
context of a regular national economic planning exercise.

On specific criteria to guide wages and prices there were marked
similarities between those enunciated in the United States and in
the United Kingdom between 1962 and 1966. But 1966 was a
bad year for them. Stronger opposition to the United States guideposts developed. The United Kingdom abandoned, at least tem-
porarily, the criteria in an effort to achieve a standstill on money
incomes. Since the criteria of an incomes policy have implications

for the distribution of incomes, some people feel it is important first to try to achieve a national consensus on a socially just distribution of incomes and to link the criteria to this consensus. France is an example of a country that has been interested recently in securing agreement and guides for the distribution of increases in income projected in the intermediate term plans.

Finally, great differences can exist on means of trying to gain compliance to the criteria. Until last year the United Kingdom had relied on moral suasion but then swung to a system of legal controls on wages and prices for a twelve-month period, although the appeal is still for a voluntary system. The United States has attempted to achieve compliance largely through a voluntary approach, but some non-compliers have nevertheless faced the possibilities of such sanctions as shifts in government purchases, manipulation of government stockpiles, anti-trust investigations, public censure for operating against the national interest in times of war in Vietnam, and changes in the degree of protection from foreign competition. In the Netherlands rigorous controls have existed over much of the postwar period, although the governmental powers under the statutory wage system have at times, as in recent years, had to give in to strong excess demand conditions in the market.

In view of this diversity of approaches it can be misleading to be too specific on what is meant by an incomes policy. But there appears to be a sufficient number of common elements in the approaches to justify talking about a species of economic policy, frequently referred to as incomes policy, that some countries have tried and that other countries have clearly not been interested in trying recently. What benefits and costs may be suggested as important to consider in evaluating it?

A variety of benefits have been suggested from an incomes policy, not all of them economic. There have been strong political and social, as well as economic, bases to an interest in it. Some that have been suggested, for example, are that it can be politically attractive as a means of reducing a government's responsibility for inflation and of helping to secure greater public support for other government programmes, that it may increase political and social stability by securing greater agreement on a socially just distribution of incomes, that it is at times a kind of mass placebo to reassure a public unduly apprehensive about inflation, or that it can shake businessmen and workers out of old attitudes and habits to provide new initiative for growth. But the main interest lies in the benefits of an incomes policy in securing directly a better control over general price movements.

The expected benefits here will be influenced by views on how money incomes and prices are determined in an economic system. Those who feel that prices and wages are very largely determined by the market forces in which businessmen and workers find themselves are likely to minimize the effect an incomes policy could or should have and to emphasize the types of policies that broadly influence the market forces. On the other hand, those who think that prices and wages are to a considerable extent independently determined by the exercise of economic power of businesses and unions and that the necessary demand conditions to permit a sustained rise in the price level without a rising unemployment of labour and capital are somehow created are likely to be more in favour of an incomes policy. But even in this latter case there may be opposition to an incomes policy and support for other means of improving the functioning of economic markets.

Without entering into the complex issues in this area it seems reasonable to point out that the overwhelming evidence from the large number of serious studies of inflation in many Western countries is that movements in monetary demand conditions have been primarily responsible for large changes in the price level. But this evidence is not, of course, inconsistent with many other factors affecting the rate of price increases at given employment levels: there is the effect on the domestic price level of a rise in foreign prices, expectations of future wage and price changes may get out of line with underlying economic conditions, movements in the consumer price index are likely to have some direct influence on wage settlements, wage or price changes in some key sectors may be interpreted as a clue, in a highly uncertain world, of changes to be expected in other sectors, conventions about major wage negotiations play a role, and concentrations of economic power in both labour and product markets mean the size and timing of many wage and price changes are not too sensitive to monetary demand conditions.

The factors over which an incomes policy might have some effect have not been set out too clearly, but several appear to have emerged in recent discussions. There is considerable enthusiasm for an incomes policy as an important educational device which would remove many of the myths in public discussions of wages and prices. It is hoped that, by setting out economically sensible rules about how wages and prices should behave, periodic inflated expectations about wages and prices can be kept under better control and that those sectors of the economy, which for a variety of reasons may be more sheltered from competitive economic forces, will nevertheless be curbed in the setting of wages and prices. Thus, in discussions of the United States wage-price guideposts much emphasis was placed on bringing under better public control certain key industries that had been charged as pattern-setters in inflation. In Canada there has been a concern this past year that some of the wage settlements—in a number of which the government has played a role—have been unrealistically high and that an incomes policy would have curbed them. A great attraction of an incomes policy to many is that it can be comprehensive in setting out rules for factor markets as well as product markets and that, particularly when there is extensive government intervention in economic markets to shore up particular groups, the policy will expose and curb the costs of such intervention.

Repeatedly, in foreign experiences, countries have been most interested in an incomes policy when severe balance-of-payments difficulties have threatened. One has only to trace the series of attempts at an incomes policy in the United Kingdom to see this point. Incomes policy has sometimes been suggested as a supplement to deflationary policies to bring about a quicker and smoother adjustment of wages and prices to a lower rate of increase, especially when it was felt there were important constraints on the use of exchange rate adjustments. In addition, under severe crisis conditions, such as in wartime or in periods when particularly large reallocations of resources were required, the exceptional strain on market mechanisms led many countries to prefer wage and price controls for a time.

A key question, however, is whether incomes policy does in fact do what it is supposed to do in moderating the rate of price increases at given employment levels or whether it has largely represented wishful thinking. This is an empirical question to which it is not easy to give a simple answer.

If the question is, "Can incomes policy have an effect?" the answer is obviously yes. Wartime wage and price controls in Canada had an effect. Controls on wages in the Netherlands have had an important effect on the timing of wage movements, although the longer-run effect is more open to question, and they failed to halt the wage explosion beginning in 1963 that sent average wages up by about 38 per cent in three years. The stricter price controls in France in 1963 had an effect. The freeze and accompanying controls on incomes and prices introduced in the United Kingdom July 1966 appear to be having an effect on the basis of available evidence. But interest has centred on the effect if much less severe sanctions were used.

In the case of the United Kingdom, an incomes policy in 1948–1950 reduced the rate of increase of wages, but the effect on prices was less clear and the policy broke down. In 1961–62 a modest decline in the rate of increase of weekly wages occurred when the Government called for a pay pause, but there is considerable doubt about whether earnings and prices were significantly influenced. Efforts to convert the pause to a longer-term policy from 1962 to 1964 are generally regarded as a failure. With the new Labour Government in the fall of 1964 a stronger effort was made to develop a voluntary incomes policy, and it received a greater backing from the Trades Union Congress than had previously been the case. There is some evidence that the rate of advance of negotiated weekly wage rates was a little slower than might otherwise have occurred, but there is a substantial difference between the wages negotiated in the major settlements and the actual movement of earnings as they are determined at the plant level in the United Kingdom, the well-known phenomenon of wage drift. The rate of increase of earnings appears to have been unaffected, advancing at a rate of over three times that proposed in the official incomes policy. To gain more effect the British Government turned last summer to strong sanctions on at least a temporary basis. The increased investment that has gone into an incomes policy in the United Kingdom recently means, however, that it is still too early to judge the future returns.

The United States is a particularly interesting case. The approach has been a largely voluntary one, but as noted above there has been the threat of penalties to non-compliers at times, and greater difficulties have emerged this past year in maintaining the guideposts. Studies point to the fact that the rate of increase of wages and prices was a little lower since the introduction of the guideposts in 1962 than might have been expected on the basis of earlier postwar economic relationships. Although a number of alternative explanations have been offered and it is clearly difficult to establish conclusively that the guideposts had a significant effect, the evidence is consistent with some effect. But, at this time, it is not entirely clear whether one should discuss the guideposts in the present or past tense.

Thus, incomes policies have been a failure at times, but they have also had an effect at other times. The evidence so far does not suggest that a successful policy will have large effects and, apart from some zealots, exponents of incomes policy generally set fairly modest aims for it. A moderation in the rate of increase of average prices of up to about one percentage point at given employment levels is a target for a successful incomes policy that one sometimes hears mentioned by economists in both the United States and the United Kingdom.

Against the assessment of the potential benefits of an incomes policy it is important, however, to set the possible economic and non-economic costs which, of course, will be influenced by the specific form the policy takes and the skill with which it is administered. There is the broad question of whether in an effort to stabilize price movements through an incomes policy a greater distortion to the allocation of economic resources will occur which will impair economic growth.

First, there has been the problem of working out criteria that are simple enough for public comprehension and for the avoidance of large loopholes in their application but are also complex enough and flexible enough to meet the varying economic situations in which they are to be applied. There has been the charge by some in the United States, for example, that the criteria used have tended to be derived from simple arithmetic truisms for yielding price stability at the aggregate or over-all economy level without sufficient regard for the complex behavioural relations at the micro level. This may be an area in which better criteria will evolve, but at this stage there is the danger either that the criteria will seem so unrealistic for individual decisions that they are disregarded or that the criteria, if applied, will impair the process of reallocating resources that are so important for growth.

Second, in implementing official criteria for incomes and prices there is the danger of discrimination. Some wage and price decisions are much easier to expose and control than others, and as a result the policy may be implemented in a discriminatory form that is not desirable on equity or economic grounds. Not only is it easier to affect some sectors, but it is also easier to bring pressure against some price increases than against cases where price decreases should occur. In Canada there has recently been the argument that an incomes policy would restrain the rate of advance of wages in the public sector, but there are limits to what can be achieved here as the United Kingdom experience in 1961–62 demonstrated. When the British Government attempted to lead the way on an incomes policy by halting wage increases in the public sector, the private sector did not follow, and a great deal of unrest built up about the unfair impact. In the United States the guideposts have been applied most vigorously in cases that would receive much national attention, and this has led to the charge that the policy has been too discriminatory in its application. Even in the Netherlands, where the policy has been much more comprehensive, the feeling that some groups were escaping the incomes policy contributed to its weakening in recent years.

Third, if the government is to formulate and implement criteria for incomes and prices, there may be a greater danger of political pressures becoming a more important influence on the wage and price structure which could raise some obvious problems.

None of these points, of course, invalidate an incomes policy from the start: the criteria need not be perfect, improvements in the criteria may develop, discrimination is not peculiar to an incomes policy among public policies, and some government involvement in wage and price decisions is an inescapable fact of economic life.

Apart from these considerations of allocation, there is the broad question of the effect of an official incomes policy on other economic policies. A government, in order to win popular support for the appropriateness of the criteria and for their implementation, will have to engage in a time-consuming selling job. The political resources for leading the country on economic policies are limited, however, and there is danger that the disproportionately large time of selling an incomes policy in relation to the potential benefits will lead to a cost in terms of not gaining public support for other policies. Thus, in the Netherlands, when strong excess demand conditions emerged in 1963, it was apparently more difficult to get public support for stronger deflationary policies because of the emphasis on incomes policy for curbing inflation. In the United Kingdom, some suggest that the continual hope for large effects from an incomes policy inhibited public support for other more fundamental policies that would have come to grips with the recurrent balance-of-payments difficulties. In addition, there is the point that if an incomes policy is not having the obvious effects promised in the government's promotion of it, the government, in order to avoid serious political embarrassment, may move towards more serious forms of control devices than were originally felt to be desirable on longer-term grounds.

Finally, an incomes policy has been viewed as bringing social benefits by achieving greater agreement on an equitable distribution of incomes and by reducing perhaps the crass materialism involved in struggles over relative incomes. But not all think the social benefits are so obvious. If there is not general agreement on the appropriateness of the criteria for wages and prices—and experience should not give us illusions about the insignificance of the problems —the implementation of official criteria may be viewed as a serious infringement on the freedom of workers and employers in making economic decisions.

Evaluations of the potential benefits and costs, not surprisingly, vary among countries and within countries over time. The particular economic circumstances and problems of the country, characteristics of labour, management, and government institutions, the form of the proposed policy, the confidence in its administration, and evidence of important alternative approaches will all affect calculations of the returns from such a policy. Undoubtedly, these factors will not remain constant in Canada over time.

It has been in periods of severe economic crisis that the gains from an incomes policy have appeared to be most attractive in relation to the costs. There have been times when market processes for allocating economic resources have been under exceptional pressures, such as in wartime or during postwar reconstructions. Under peacetime conditions, experiences in other countries indicate that the following situation has produced strongest pressures for an incomes policy: a serious balance-of-payments problem has emerged, direct measures to deal with the balance of payments, such as an exchange rate adjustment, have been viewed as unacceptable or inadequate, and more restrictive monetary and fiscal policies have been strongly opposed on the grounds of the costs in terms of lower employment levels. Particularly in a crisis situation it is easier to rally voluntary support for an incomes policy. Thus, there may be times in Canada in the future when it will be useful to use incomes policy as a short-run emergency device to help during a period of rearrangement of more basic policies to deal with the sources of a crisis.

At the present time, however, the principal question is whether it would be attractive under more normal conditions and over the longer run to try to develop and implement a set of official criteria for incomes and prices. As I have stated there are important arguments on both sides of this question. It is not at all difficult to wax eloquent on the attractions of an incomes policy for Canada; the really troublesome issues lie in specifying appropriate criteria and in securing their implementation. In view of the difficulties that have emerged this past year in both the United States and the United Kingdom with maintaining in the longer-run criteria for wages and prices, it is important to watch if improvements in them will emerge and to consider if there is a more appropriate set that could be developed in Canada now.

Canada is probably not very fertile ground for cultivating a serious form of incomes policy at this stage of her economic history in relation to that of a number of other countries. The greater decentralization of labour and management institutions in Canada than in many other Western countries limits more the role that leaders of labour and management institutions could play in enlisting unified support of workers and businessmen. The large regional economic differences within Canada and the degree of economic integration of factor and product markets with those of the United States would complicate the problems of formulating and applying criteria. Public acceptance of official criteria will be influenced by the extent of national economic cohesion. The Dutch postwar reconstruction problems, the series of British balance-of-payments crises, and the United States military involvements abroad have all been factors in helping to unify past support for incomes policies in those countries. With respect to the government's power to implement the criteria through penalizing or threatening to penalize those who do not comply, there are the well-known constitutional issues in Canada that divide the federal and provincial jurisdictions in a number of areas relevant for an incomes policy and that would thus impose much greater limitations on the room for central government action than in other Western countries, including the United States.

Finally, it is important to consider if an investment in alternative approaches could yield a higher return and be more feasible in the Canadian environment. Presumably, as in the past in all countries, governments in Canada will find it useful from time to time to exhort people to better performances on wages and prices. But are there newer, more specific approaches? Important steps in the area of wage-price policies need not begin with a government commitment to implement an official, economy-wide set of criteria for money incomes and prices. It is difficult to know at this time what the future form of their policies will be, but in the past the Swedes have strongly denied that their efforts in the area of wage-price policies should be described as incomes policy. The reason is that there has been a distinctive approach which in the past has not come at the problems through a set of specific government criteria for incomes and prices. It is the latter that has characterized what have been called incomes policies in recent years. But, if it is more convenient to describe anything in the broad area of wage-price policies as an incomes policy, then it is important to distinguish carefully the quite different approaches that may be taken.

It seems to me that there are three main sources of benefits from new steps in the field of wage and price policies. The first is to improve the factual and analytical bases to our understanding of the determinants of money incomes and prices. The second is to raise the level of economic discussions in the country in order to try to remove some of the myths surrounding controversies over wage and price developments, to help prevent expectations from getting out of line with underlying economic conditions, to provide good critical debate on the current appropriateness of institutional arrangements and concentrations of economic power that affect money incomes and prices, and to stimulate means of achieving greater agreement on the principles that should govern the distribution of incomes. The third is to seek improvements in the use of the great power of governments not only in developing broad aggregative policies affecting the general movement of money incomes and prices, but also in developing specific policies for the wage settlements in which governments play a role, for the control of abuses of economic power in product, labour, and capital markets, for facilitating economic adjustment processes where wage and price signals are inadequate, and for reducing the adverse distributive effects of both unemployment and general price changes.

The alternatives here are diverse. They suffer in comparison with an approach that begins with a set of government criteria for incomes and prices, because they are not as neat and as easy to organize. But perhaps the economic system is not that tidy. There is the argument that the alternatives might not have as great an effect; this is perhaps true at least in the short run. They need to be considered, however, on the basis of both costs and benefits. Experiences in other countries—in the Netherlands, the United Kingdom, the United States—indicate the strong pressures to modify the initial, simpler approaches to a longer-run incomes policy in the face of the complexities of the economic system.

Among the specific things that might be suggested here are, first, the development of annual debates on current and expected income and price developments and on appropriate national targets for wages and prices. Second, means of stimulating better critical reviews of patterns and special problems in wage and price changes could be proposed. A useful catalyst in my view would be an independent body that could delve into controversial issues in the area of incomes, productivity, and prices, if it could be conceived in an appropriate form. Such a body might find it desirable to suggest criteria or guidelines for wages and prices which would not need to commit governments to their defence but which would help induce labour, business, and governments to rethink constantly their wage and price policies. Its greatest service would be that of providing more information and better analyses of wage and price issues to the public that ultimately controls the decisions of its leaders. Third, more attention could be given to developing better machinery within governments for co-ordinating the complex array of government measures which influence relative as well as average income and price movements. Governments now exert a pervasive direct and indirect influence on wages and prices; the potential returns are high from improved processes of public decision-making that would permit better over-all pictures of how the many bits and pieces of governmental action do and could fit together.

Discussion

M. W. FARRELL

F. C. BURNET

ROBERT SAUVÉ

WILLIAM DODGE

M. W. FARRELL: The Manpower and Social Affairs Division of the Organization for Economic Co-operation and Development invited Canada to provide a mission to study incomes policy and labour-market operations in Great Britain and Sweden. As background, official circles in Canada had been observing with particular interest the efforts of several European countries that were attempting to restrain wage and price movements through an official incomes policy. The ministers of the twenty-one OECD countries have committed their governments to attaining a 50 per cent growth in their economies in the decade between 1960 and 1970, while attaining a good and balanced performance in three main areas of economic policy: economic growth, balance-of-payments equilibrium, and price stability. Sweden, like Canada, has an official incomes policy in which government intervention has been confined to orthodox fiscal policy and supporting monetary action. Great Britain, by contrast, in its incomes policy has gone a considerable distance in using direct measures of price restraint and wage and profits control.

My major interest and background of experience ran more towards the incomes policies phase of the joint mission. It is essential at the very start to draw attention to the long-term objectives of incomes policy, as distinct from the short-term emergency of mastering a serious balance-of-payments problem. Indeed, the major attention and efforts of Britain's economic policy in 1966 and 1967 continue to centre on the elimination of the balance-of-payments deficit and the re-establishment of confidence in the foreign exchange value of the pound sterling. Until the short-term crisis is satisfactorily resolved, long-range policies are set aside for some future date. Unfortunately, however, some of the short-term measures are intensifying the longer-range problems.

The background of Britain's long-range economic problems and its incomes policy is very complex and includes conflicting objectives. To attempt to summarize and to prescribe solutions on the basis of a one-week assessment is bound to involve some broad generalities, but some of our findings are important.

Britain continues to be one of the world's great financial centres, handling the foreign exchange reserve balances of the sterling area. Many international loans are arranged through London, while for many of the major raw materials of world trade, Britain is still the centre at which prices are determined. Britain has a great and valued position which depends on world confidence in the soundness and the stability of the pound sterling. One objective of the nation's economic policy is to support the foreign exchange value of the currency, first through short-term assistance from the International Monetary Fund and foreign central banks, and ultimately through a strong balance-of-payments position without the need for emergency support.

Another objective is to be a part of the large economic communities so as to share in bigger consuming markets, to share in the economies of large-scale production based on these markets, and to provide the impetus for new technological breakthroughs. However, now that the tariffs have been eliminated in the European Free Trade Association, in which Britain is the largest member, the initiative has been taken to join the larger, the wealthier, and the more industrialized European Economic Community, both to add competitive pressures to British industry and labour and to offer the attraction of larger markets. A world financial centre becomes progressively weaker unless it reflects a strongly competitive and large scale industrial base, and that base would be much more solid if Britain were a part of the EEC.

A third goal of the British has been to divide the current flow of the national income more towards consumption at the expense of capital investment generally, and particularly from the wealthier towards the lower income levels. The administration of this objective seems to be a matter of degree of emphasis between the major political parties, with one party looking more severely at wage increases and the other watching more suspiciously the actual or potential price increases. There was, for example, an "early-warning" arrangement on price increases well before the recent era of wage-price freezes. But price changes, dividend increases, and wage increases are now all under the watchful eyes of the National Board for Prices and Income.

A final major objective is to encourage more rapid adoption of new technology in industry, to tie wage increases more closely to productivity improvements, and generally to stir both management and labour into a more receptive attitude towards change and productivity improvement.

The longer-term goals of the British incomes policy were overshadowed by the balance-of-payments crisis which developed in 1966. This forced the Government to undertake emergency measures which took priority over the longer-run instruments. In plain language, domestic demand for goods, services, and investment funds was to be reduced, imports were to decline and exports increase, and capital export was to be diminished.

The British tackled the short-term problem with determination and a wide variety of instruments. On July 20, 1966, a wage-price freeze was instituted for six months, with the official but slightly reluctant concurrence of the Confederation of British Industries and the Trades Union Congress. For the subsequent six months, a period of "severe restraint" was to apply in which distress cases of wage increases, of price adjustment, and of deferred productivity agreements on wages were permissible. In September 1966 wage deductions were started under a selective employment tax which was intended to discourage employment in service industries and to divert labour to manufacturing. Tight money and credit were applied to the economy by the Bank of England. Commodity imports were put under some restraint by a 10 per cent tariff surcharge on imports (other than foods and raw materials). Incidentally, the surcharge came to an end on November 30, 1966, through pressures of the EFTA partners and other countries in GATT.

Modest tax relief was also granted on corporate income derived from export trade expansion.

It must be said that some improvements have resulted from the emergency measures: price increases have been restrained to the small amounts permitted for more costly imported materials and tax increments, wage increases have been kept down to very moderate proportions, based to some extent on shifts to higher paid skills, and imports of commodities have levelled off, subject to a moderate surge when the surcharges came off. Nonetheless, it is difficult to reduce imports when Britain needs to bring in machinery incorporating modern technology and when much manufacturing operates from imported raw materials. The foreign exchange reserves of the Bank of England have been increasing, and it may indeed be true that Britain will be able to relax its emergency balance-of-payments measures at the end of 1967 on the strength of having sufficient reserves.

Nevertheless, considerable distortions have resulted in the British economy. The monetary and credit restraint has hit at domestic buying of durable consumer goods, notably automobiles, resulting in plant layoffs. The efforts of the Board of Trade to encourage business capital investment in the less prosperous areas have stalled in spite of a late 1966 programme of incentive grants from the Treasury amounting to 45 per cent of the cost of such investment for most of Britain and to 25 per cent of the capital outlay for southeast England outside of London. The prospective business capital investment for 1967 will be lower than 1966 by something between 10 and 25 per cent. This will depress construction and heavy industry without offering short term hopes for a compensatory export expansion.

The other desirable long-term measures to stimulate the British economy will take time, patience, and hard work to accomplish. For example, the studies and the reports of the Prices and Incomes Board point the way to changes in marketing institutions, in labour practices, in technology, and in management methods. The execution of their suggestions will take time and in some cases may be thwarted by opposition or indifference.

The industrial training levy scheme under which industries receive grants for training their employees in new skills or higher skills will show its results only gradually. The traditional view that Britain has had a surplus in labour supply stands in the way of acceptance of labour-saving practices that are more readily used in the United States, Canada, or Sweden, which generally have labour shortages. The answer to this protectiveness towards labour supply undoubtedly lies in the expansion of markets and a greater regard for capital investment and high productivity as the method and the partnership out of which higher living standards develop.

It is expecting too much of British entry into the EEC to anticipate an easy and early change of traditional patterns, even though "shock treatment" was frequently mentioned in the course of our visit. It should also be expected that the dismantling of wage and price controls will release certain repressed inflation. Nevertheless, some forms of an incomes policy are likely to be a part of Britain's economic policy until the fears of inflation and deflation and of recurrent balance-of-payments crises are laid to rest.

The lessons for Canada from Britain's experience in a formal incomes policy are not too clear, as the circumstances are decidedly different. Britain is a strongly centralized economy with a chronic problem in its balance of payments, along with other features of a high reliance on international trade, relatively abundant labour, few indigenous natural resources, and slow growth in capital investment. The British experience would not of itself support the case for a formal incomes policy for Canada.

F. C. BURNET: It has been said that Sweden does not have an incomes policy. This is technically correct when measured against the official Organization for Economic Co-operation and Development definition of incomes policy, which implies a policy that is government directed to influence wage and price movements and which is based on voluntary guides. In my view this is a mere technicality in definition, for, in fact, Sweden very diligently pursues an incomes policy through the private institutions of labour and management and by methods which in some senses involve a high degree of compulsion or at least coercion.

As a prelude to understanding the Swedish version of incomes policy it is useful, I think, to note certain general features of

Swedish economic organization, objectives, and attitudes which differ significantly from Canadian arrangements. It is generally accepted that the Canadian economic system is a mixture of private and state or socialistic enterprise. The Swedish economy is also characterized by a mixture of capitalistic and socialistic concepts, but with a difference. On the production side Sweden seems to be even more heavily oriented to free-enterprise concepts than we are. The resulting product is, however, then distributed according to socialistic precepts to a greater extent than has been deemed acceptable in Canada thus far. To elaborate, over 90 per cent of Swedish industry is privately owned, but of greater significance even than this statistic is the marked degree to which the allocation of resources and the operation of industry is governed by the operation of the market place, in the classic free enterprise tradition. Four examples will illustrate the point.

(1) Sweden is one of the lowest tariff countries in the world and is favourably disposed to even lower tariffs on a reciprocal basis. The Swedes do not attempt to build their enterprises behind the protection of a tariff wall, but insist that their industries survive or not according to their competitive ability in world markets. Neither are the Swedes disposed to support weak or ailing industries with other forms of subsidy. Currently, for example, the textile industry is having difficulty meeting foreign competition in Sweden. The Swedes are apparently prepared to let this industry die and to transfer its labour and other resources to other enterprises where there is a competitive advantage or at least competitive equality.

(2) In marked contrast to Canada and the United States, there is no anti-trust or combines legislation in Sweden. Indeed, "bigness" is recognized as a key to competitive efficiency, and mergers are encouraged to this end. Consumer interests, it is felt, are adequately protected by low tariffs and the resulting threat or fact of foreign competition if prices of domestic producers are set too high.

(3) The pursuit of efficiency in production carries through to the plant floor, and there is little or no evidence of demarcation problems between crafts or trade-union groupings such as seem to hamper the British and others. Similarly, Sweden seems to have a lower tolerance than we do for work sharing or protection of out-moded jobs, no doubt because of the fact that there is a shortage

of labour and that rather elaborate schemes have been devised to retrain and reallocate displaced workers to productive enterprises.

(4) Finally, the Swedish policy for regionally depressed areas is not to attract industry into such areas by tax policy or other subsidies, but rather to move the people out. Economic considerations take precedence over social considerations in this situation, and the trend is towards transfer of people from the rural north to the more industrialized urban areas of the south.

Having directed its efforts to maximize production and productivity efficiency, the Swedes then seek to level out the distribution of income to a greater extent than we do. Tax policies and social-welfare objectives are applied to this end. Universal state pension schemes provide pensions on retirement at about two-thirds of income prior to retirement for the great bulk of the population, and there are highly developed schemes to provide universal medical service, free education through university, free government retraining of unemployed, including payment of trainees on a comparatively generous scale during the training period, unemployment insurance, and so on. The impression is created that there are probably fewer poor in Sweden proportionately and also fewer well-to-do or wealthy than is the case in Canada.

The mechanism for bargaining in Sweden is based on the fact that labour and management are both organized into very strong central federations, each of which can exert considerable direct control over its members. These central federations negotiate the limits of wage increases, with the government assisting by providing statistical information and information of proposed monetary and fiscal policies. Bargaining in Sweden is largely a matter of conditioning public expectations. The ultimate persuader is the strike or lockout, and the unusual feature here is the ability and willingness of the employers to use the lockout on an industry or even national scale. When agreement is reached between the central labour-management bodies, negotiations proceed at regional and local levels on the specific distribution of the agreed upon increase.

Enforcement of the wage limits is a joint responsibility of the two central federations. It is clear, however, that the employers are the stronger and have assumed more responsibility for enforcement of the bargaining than has the labour side. For example, a recalcitrant employer who exceeded the limits of the wage bargain could be faced with fines by the employers' association and a boycott by other employers; a recalcitrant local union which sought to break the limits would not only face a lockout in its particular plant, but would also probably find other local unions in its industry also locked out by employers.

When one adds to this structure the fact that there is in Sweden a small and homogeneous population, a high degree of labour-management co-operation, a unitary state as opposed to our Canadian federal state, and a generally higher degree of economic sophistication among the population generally, it seems fair to say that the probability of controlling the rate of increase in incomes within the agreed limits should be very high indeed. In fact, the conditions are almost ideal.

In the face of these conditions, the results achieved are somewhat surprising and, in my view, lend considerable support to the school of thought which looks sceptically at the practicality of an incomes policy. Over the ten-year period that the Swedish system has operated, the agreed upon increases have averaged something around 3 per cent per year, but the actual increase in wages and salaries each year has been about twice that amount. Some of this additional increase may be attributable to upgrading of skills through reallocation of resources to more productive fields, but most of the excess is due to the phenomenon known as "wage drift."

About two-thirds of Swedish blue-collar workers are on some form of piece-work or incentive rate. While individual managements and unions stay within the wage bargain reached by the central federations, what seems to happen is that, under the pressures of full employment, employers are willing to allow incentive and piece-rate standards to loosen, thereby providing employees an additional, unofficial increase. One of our informants indicated that virtually all of the annual increase in Swedish productivity is going to the blue-collar worker through this avenue.

This is not to say, of course, that the Swedish system has failed. On the contrary, the system has contributed substantially to labour peace, and the country has been relatively free of major disputes for many years. In addition, insofar as control of incomes and therefore of prices is concerned, while Sweden is concerned about its price level and problems of inflation, its actual rate of inflation is still below that of Germany, England, and the other European nations with whom it has its chief customer-supplier relationships. On the other hand, Swedish prices and costs are moving at a faster rate than those of Canada, where there is no incomes policy, or the United States, where the policy is largely one of ineffectual exhortation except in certain price situations.

There are other problems beginning to emerge under the Swedish arrangements, which are also attributable to wage drift. As indicated, wage-drift benefits those blue-collar workers who are on incentive pay systems, while the white-collar or professional workers do not benefit. As a result, there are strained relations between the labour groups which represent each of these classifications. The fact that teachers, for example, do not "benefit" from wage drift was the cause of the recent teachers' strike in Sweden. To restore their relative pay position, the teachers' union struck against the guidelines which had been agreed to by the other unions. The teachers' strike was opposed by the Government, which was the employer in this instance, and also did not have the sympathy of the bulk of the trade-union movement, most of whom did not accept the argument of the teachers that they should maintain their relative position by an additional increase to compensate for the lack of wage drift. On the contrary, the other labour groups felt that the steady narrowing of the income gap between the blue-collar workers and the professional people was a socially desirable result, entirely consistent with the objectives of the Social Democratic party.

On balance, the results of Swedish efforts to control incomes have at best achieved only partial success. Whether they are worth the effort or not is a matter for Swedish decision in the Swedish context of affairs, and the question of interest to us is the extent to which their methods could be practically applied in Canada. I should like simply to offer two opinions to sum up my impressions on this question:

(1) Surface similarities between Sweden and Canada as two small, northern trading nations are deceptive. There are in fact fundamental differences in economic organization and attitudes, political and social objectives, size and nature of population, and

government and labour-management structures, which would make it quite impractical for us to try to adopt the Swedish labour-relations system or its procedures aimed at controlling incomes.

(2) The limited success of Swedish efforts to control incomes under the almost ideal conditions prevailing in that country does not encourage me to believe that an incomes policy in Canada would be successful. Rather, our efforts should be directed to improving our productive capacity by upgrading the skills of our work force by providing conditions for sound capital investment, by refining our skills in applying governmental monetary and fiscal controls, and by reconciling as best we can the conflicting aims of price stability and full employment.

ROBERT SAUVÉ: We were sent to England and Sweden to study prices and incomes policy and labour-market operations in order to determine whether they might be applicable either in whole or in part in Canada. The task was a difficult one, partly because of many domestic economic problems in Canada, such as American investment and conflicts arising out of the federal structure of government, which are not present in either England or Sweden.

In England, with their prices and incomes policy, the British are trying to overcome their balance-of-payments problems and to increase productivity. Dr. Phelps Brown of the London School of Economics succinctly described the problem when he said the British people were living in a "cost-plus" society: as employers are taxed they increase prices, workers then ask for higher wages, and the vicious circle of increasing costs begins. He felt that the only way to overcome this situation was to change the attitude of the British people and was quite optimistic that this could be done. I personally was pessimistic about the prospects for a change. Moreover, I felt that the British were taking a short-term view of the question and that perhaps panic had led them to resort to unduly severe measures.

We often asked in Britain: "If a one- or two-year collective agreement due to expire in August 1967 was frozen, how long could the workers be expected to refrain from demanding further concessions?" We did not receive any specific or sufficient answer to this question. We can merely summarize by suggesting that it appears that the British will now live under a "voluntary-compulsory" system. I wondered if the freeze bill and the severe restraint with the conditions imposed would not be prolonged for another period. Government intervention is contrary to the traditional British thinking, but opposition to the policy is relatively mild because management appears weak, and the structure of the labour movement seems old-fashioned, and based mainly on crafts.

In Sweden we came to several conclusions. Manpower policies appeared effective, but it was obvious that management was the policy-making body. There are no work stoppages, except on renewal of contracts, and fringe benefits are provided by government legislation, thus eliminating the need for negotiation between labour and management.

There is a great fear in the LO, TCO, and SACO (the initials for the three major Swedish federations of labour, representing both blue- and white-collar workers, almost solely white-collar workers, and professional workers, respectively) of government intervention. This fear is weakening the unions and the last collective agreement would be difficult for us to accept because it is a three-year agreement which did not respect the mandate given by the workers. It was signed before the expiry of the old contract and was not submitted to the union membership for ratification. This led to great turmoil. At least one group on the workers' side wanted to negotiate something over and above the national agreement— and in my opinion they had no other choice—but they did not have the support of their organizations. The SAF (the central federation of Swedish employers) refused to sign the collective agreement until the dissident group came in.

Moreover, even to arrive at the last central agreement the LO had to threaten to abandon overtime. The SAF replied by a threat of a lockout, and a settlement was immediately reached. How long will the rank-and-file member remain silent in the face of such strong management control?

From my observations I concluded that Britain seems to be in a fight to survive and Sweden is no paradise, but is probably a better place for employers than employees to live.

WILLIAM DODGE: The important thing to bear in mind in discussions of this kind is that no two countries have precisely similar histories, structures, or economic problems, and variations in size, population, location, attitudes, national character, political orientation, and resources influence policy decisions and the methods of solving particular economic problems. Policies which are practical and acceptable in one country may be totally irrelevant in another.

These differences make comparisons between countries difficult. Canadians are often envious of the Swedish system of enlightened labour-management relations and incomes policy and assume that if only labour, or management, or both had more sense here, we could do the same. We think it is simply a matter of good will or good sense and too often fail to realize that the environment is a really critical factor.

There is value in a trip such as we have participated in. We were at least able to ask how particular countries tackle the problems peculiar to them given their existing economic, social, and political setting: Do they act promptly, wisely and boldly? Do they relate solutions to immediate problems to the long-term consequences? How is public support won for essential measures? How and by whom are the critical decisions made? Are the solutions applied logical and effective? Can the observer arrive at an objective evaluation of the measures taken?

I am sure no one here expects us to answer any of these questions conclusively with respect to manpower and incomes policies in Britain and Sweden. All we can give are our impressions. These, very briefly, were mine.

The impression I gained of Britain's manpower programmes are that they are pitifully inadequate to meet the country's manpower needs. Although Britain has suffered from a shortage of manpower almost continuously since the Second World War (with an unemployment rate of 1 to 2½ per cent during most of the period), the programmes designed to alleviate the shortage, particularly in skilled classifications, have been poorly planned and are ineffective.

Although it was admitted that one of the causes of inflation in Britain has been the shortage of skilled manpower, capital expenditures on training facilities by the government over the three-year period ending April 1, 1966, amounted to about £5 million, and trainee accommodations have only risen from 2,490 places to 5,961 places during that period. This is in relation to a labour force of almost 25 million. In terms of the need, it is a ridiculously small contribution.

The employment service in Britain has the same complaint as ours has had here for many years: it is tied to the payment of insurance benefits, or the dole, as it is often called. What is worse, it is also tied to a number of other public benefits, with employment offices serving as distribution centres for food tokens, passport application offices, and various other purposes. Only 25 per cent of total placements pass through the employment service, and fee charging employment agencies seem to be operating everywhere.

In spite of conditions of over-all full employment, some regions suffer from unemployment. In a country as small and compact as the United Kingdom, the problem of mobility, of bringing unemployed persons into the areas where labour shortages exist, should be relatively easily overcome. Unfortunately, a severe shortage of housing has effectively nullified the quite advanced forms of mobility assistance.

No statistics appeared to be available on immigration and emigration as they affect the manpower situation. Board of Trade officials said they have not regarded migration as having a relation to manpower needs.

I believe that neglect of the role played by manpower policies in the determination of prices and productivity and in turn the country's competitive situation has been a considerable factor in the development of the current economic crisis in Britain. I thought it was significant that this did not seem to be widely recognized among those with whom we discussed the economic situation, with the exception of one very frustrated official.

My personal view is that unless Britain can develop a sound labour-market policy and provide adequate facilities to put it into effect, the present "short-term" economic problems may well turn into "long-term" difficulties. While some patching is being done, no fundamental changes in policy seem to be under consideration at present.

The Swedes, on the other hand, told us that an economist had said recently that it was no solution for Britain's problems to emulate Sweden's labour-market policy, because Sweden has similar problems which her labour-market policy could not solve.

I find it difficult to accept that statement. In the first place, while Sweden has indeed a labour shortage, greatly intensified in the highly industrialized areas (the unemployment rate was 0.8 per cent in mid-October 1966) and some inflationary pressure is evident, there are no signs of a severe national economic crisis. The most pressing problem is housing and this has, as in Britain, aggravated manpower mobility difficulties.

Generally, however, the Swedes have elevated their manpower programmes to the status of an art. As they put it, the main task of manpower policy is to assist people to adjust to the new conditions of employment which are occurring every day. They know that all their manpower problems cannot be solved through labour-market programmes, and that effective fiscal and monetary policies are the basis of economic growth and stability, but they have built an efficient and vigorous labour-market operation which is capable of eliminating many of the structural bottlenecks we and other nations suffer from in the promotion of the effective use of our manpower resources.

As we turn back to the matter of incomes policy and its relevance to the situation in Britain, I feel a strong disposition to applaud the position taken by the Government, despite some reservations about its practicability and some doubts about its long-term effectiveness. A sincere attempt has been made, I believe, to provide affirmative answers to some of the questions posed earlier: the Government acted promptly, boldly, and probably wisely. They have clearly considered the long-term consequences of their actions and have effectively won public support for their policy. The machinery for decision-making is intelligently conceived and democratic in structure.

Britain's incomes policy stems from a joint statement of intent signed on December 16, 1964, by representatives of the Government, employers' organizations, and the Trades Union Congress. This statement included the following declaration: "We must take urgent and vigorous action (*i*) to raise productivity throughout industry and commerce; (*ii*) to keep increases in total money incomes in line with increases in real national output; (*iii*) to maintain a stable general price level."

The employers and the union representatives undertook to co-operate with machinery designed to "(*i*) keep under review the general movements of prices and of money incomes of all kinds, (*ii*) examine particular cases in order to advise whether or not the behaviour of prices or of wages, salaries and other money incomes is in the national interest as defined by the Government after consultation with management and unions."

On April 8, 1965, the National Board for Prices and Incomes was created and began a series of intensive studies of particular price and income movements. At the time of our visit, it had completed twenty-seven such studies, thirteen on prices and fourteen on money incomes. The Board publishes its findings but has no power to enforce them. It depends upon the voluntary co-operation of managements and unions to carry out its investigations and upon public sentiment to make its recommendations effective.

This was the situation which prevailed until the Government, confronted with the balance-of-payments crisis of last year, introduced a measure known as the "Prices and Incomes Standstill" on July 20, 1966. This standstill was to be in effect until December 31, 1966, and was to be followed by a six-months period of "severe restraint." The effect of this order has been that recommendations of the Board, which depended previously upon voluntary acceptance by the employers and unions concerned, became mandatory and are likely to continue to enjoy that status until the period of "severe restraint" has been lifted. Even before the standstill went into effect, the policy had received a substantial degree of acceptance from management and labour. In the twenty-seven cases reported upon by the Board, only one management group and a section of one union were cited as cases of non-co-operation. Furthermore, both management and labour have agreed to set up "early warning" or internal vetting procedures through which price increases and wage claims must pass before being formally announced. A remarkable degree of co-operation with this procedure had been achieved.

I do not know whether or not this plan will succeed in keeping money incomes in line with productivity increases or maintaining stable price levels, much less solve Britain's economic crisis. Unions are sceptical about pressures designed to keep wages in check. For example, they see demands for wage increases as a means of forcing management to improve technology and increase productivity. Management also naturally resents interference with their right to set the prices of their products.

The Board takes its activities very seriously in spite of these reservations, and while it depends upon voluntary co-operation and the pressure of public opinion to make its recommendations effective, it truly believes itself to be fulfilling its assigned role of gaining general acceptance of the fact that the price determined by a firm or group of firms or a wage negotiated by a union affects others outside the membership of the bodies concerned.

I think it is an intelligent application of a modified incomes policy within the context of Britain's current economic problem. Will it work? No one knows yet, but if it does, the experiment in Britain may have as important an influence upon price and incomes policy in the Western developed countries as Sweden's enlightened policies have had upon labour-market programmes and labour-management relations.

Swedish trade unionists contend that Sweden does not have an incomes policy. But, Sweden has indeed an incomes policy. An incomes policy does not necessarily imply control mechanisms or wage- and price-fixing bodies. As soon as a government introduces a graduated income tax and social-security measures for the purpose of transferring incomes from one group to another, it has set out upon the road towards an incomes policy. Anti-monopoly legislation, minimum wage laws, boards governing the charges for utilities, and subsidized housing all form a body of policy which is intended to affect the distribution of incomes between the various factors of production. A rounded incomes policy would of course necessarily involve in addition some way of tying wages to price and productivity changes and to policies conducive to expanded trade, economic growth, and full employment. By that definition I think Sweden has an exceedingly effective and intelligent incomes policy.

Representatives of Swedish Government, labour, and management recognize that economic stability depends upon a sound system of incomes formation. They stress the connection between incomes formation in the export industry and in the economy as a whole. When the economic situation permits the export industry to concede substantial wage increases through normal collective bargaining, there is a tendency for these increases to spread over the rest of the economy, including industries less capable of absorbing the increased labour costs. The inflationary pressures thus induced in turn undermine the external trade position.

Something like that has been happening lately in Sweden. In 1965, Sweden experienced a substantial unfavourable balance of trade. This was corrected somewhat in 1966, but the 1966 agreements were expected to bring new complications into the cost situation. An interest in more formal incomes policy is consequently being awakened in some quarters. But there is still a great deal of reliance on informal procedures. The accepted approach is that it is up to labour and management to work out a wages policy based upon the behaviour of the economy as a whole. It is the role of government to control the general economic climate in which these negotiations take place and to maintain it in a state of health.

Sweden has strong organizations of both employers and labour. They are very well informed on economic trends, and they are both well supplied with excellent economists whose approach to economic problems is very sophisticated. Government officials are in constant communication with both employers and unions on the state of the economy, and there is much informal discussion of economic matters. As one authority remarked: "Sweden is a small country and the Minister of Labour, the President of the LO and the President of the SAF are personal friends." They see no need to set up machinery for dealing with the special question of incomes.

No one has yet developed a truly effective incomes policy, and no one is likely to do so in the foreseeable future. The Swedes have economic problems just like everyone else and they do not have all the answers either. But my own impression is that all of the present features of incomes-determination machinery in Sweden add up to a formidable body of policy which is superior to anything so far devised anywhere else.

SESSION SUMMARY, *by V. W. Bladen*

We all agree that policy, or the objectives of policy, should be to ensure that wages and prices behave as we want them to. The problem is, of course, to determine how far we have achieved this and what methods have been used, and should be used, to improve our performance in this respect.

We have been discussing three methods: one involves a good deal of compulsion and the policing power of the state, the second involves a considerable use of persuasion, and the third relates to the serious use of the instruments which we pretend we use—fiscal and monetary policy. My worry about the first two devices is largely that they divert our government and our politicians from their real responsibility of making a serious attempt to achieve these objectives within the framework of a free market through properly co-ordinated monetary and fiscal policy. Until this has been really tried and failed, I do not want to see us trying other ways to enable the politicians to get out of the troubles that they have got into through a failure to behave as they should.

Of course in the process certain additional measures are needed. I am very interested in the extremely strong emphasis that has been put on manpower management. I would like to urge that consideration be given to the role of unemployment insurance. If unemployment benefits were paid at a rate that was reasonable, and particularly if they had some relationship to the previous earnings of those unemployed instead of being a minimum equal amount for everybody, and if serious programmes of retraining and relocation were undertaken, much of the stigma of unemployment would be eliminated.

Given policies such as these I think it would not be so difficult for the Government to attempt to achieve both price stability and high level employment. They would not always have to choose to let prices go up lest there be a slight increase on unemployment. In saying this, of course, I am taking a line which Professor Harry Johnson took recently when he said that the argument for attempting to avoid economic instability is largely based on the undesirability of the social consequences of instability, particularly of unemployment on the one hand and inflation on the other. If, as he said, a sociably undesirable degree of instability is regarded as economically unavoidable, its effects could be mitigated by a greater generosity towards its victims.

If I may refer to another aspect of the problem, I suggest that we all think about one very serious problem. We were told that various incomes policies have had some effect, but when members of the OECD were talking about this effect it seems that they were talking about the effect on wages or prices. I want them to consider the effect on productivity. Suppose the Government has persuaded union leaders to get their members to accept a wage settlement that seems extremely unsatisfactory to the bulk of these members. Suppose they in fact do loyally stay at or go back to work. Will they work as hard as they would if they had in fact achieved what they considered a reasonable objective in the way of a wage increase? Can we be sure that in controlling wages we are not sometimes raising wage costs, even though we are lowering wage rates, or preventing wage rates from increasing as fast as they otherwise would. I think this is a vitally important question. I do not think people have been addressing themselves to it. I wish they would.

Of course I am allergic to intervention, that is, to any more intervention than is necessary. I am also allergic to this business of persuasion. I do not believe in it, and I rather dislike it. My attitude is best summed up in the remarks of a very great English economist, Sir Denis Robertson: "Persuasiveness and persuadability are valuable things; but, like most valuable things, limited in supply. It is the duty of society to create a framework . . . and to operate a regime of incentives and dis-incentives which will prevent these precious qualities of persuasiveness and persuadability from being wastefully squandered through being set tasks which it is outside their compass to perform."

In the emergency of England in a sterling crisis I think even Sir Denis would agree that some use of persuasiveness and persuadability was appropriate. I am not so sure that he would agree in the conditions of the United States in recent months. I do not believe that we in Canada should relieve the Government and the Bank of Canada of the clear obligation to direct their monetary and fiscal policies to achieve the objectives we share by saying "if you fail we will use a lot of persuasion. We'll try to persuade people not to do that which is profitable to them. We'll try to persuade unions not to ask for the wages that they clearly would get if they pressed." I do not believe in that way of running economic affairs.

THE GOVERNMENT AND
WAGE-PRICE-PROFIT
RELATIONS

INTRODUCTION, *by Dr. C. T. Bissell*

It used to be said of Mitchell Sharp that he was too academic, too devoted to the processes of rational argument, to succeed in politics. It is therefore reassuring to us in the University that he has been able to secure such an influential position without any diminution of his rationality, but perhaps with some development of the assertive mode in the delivery of those arguments. It is reassuring to know that there are men of academic bent in the Government, for universities must now make their case to government, and we need understanding and occasionally a tax point.

You will notice that Mr. Sharp's paper is posed dramatically between the statement of the problem and what I gather will be a proper solution. He is not expected to provide the answers, but we shall not be disappointed, nor indeed surprised, if he does.

The Government of Canada Looks at Wage-Price-Profit Relations

THE HONOURABLE
MITCHELL SHARP

The job of government in meeting problems of inflation is more difficult, at least more far-reaching, than that confronted by other members of the community. I do not mean to say that the problems encountered by different groups in the community are less difficult or less trying, but each group naturally has looked at solutions from its own point of view, without dwelling on, or perhaps identifying, the national consequences. The wage-earner, or retired person, tries to raise his income, once prices have begun to rise, to re-establish his former position or perhaps even to improve it. The businessman attempts usually to raise his prices to cover rising costs, to the extent he can, while at the same time he works to lower his costs through improvements in productivity.

Governments, on the other hand, given the multitude of objectives with which they must be concerned, cannot rely on single or even simple solutions. Economic matters are so interrelated both within the country and now even among countries of the world, that every government measure must take into account the potential effect on employment, economic growth, distribution of wealth, the country's international competitive position, and its balance of payments. All of these matters are interrelated in ways which create problems for the policy-maker.

Let me give you an example. When Canadian prices rise more rapidly than those outside Canada, our international competitive position is threatened, and it becomes more difficult for Canadians to sell their products abroad. The result is that there will be an effect on the balance of payments which must be considered. If the cause of the inflation is one of excess demand and if the people want and are able to buy more than the country can produce efficiently, then the government must, if it is to do its job properly, tighten fiscal policy. It will, at the same time, of course, try to increase productive capacity, but this involves programmes whose very nature can show results only for longer periods of time. In meeting the immediate problem, the government must reduce excess demand either by reducing its expenditures or raising its taxes. Either course contains obvious political problems. Reducing expenditures may involve spending less either on measures which will improve economic performance or those which will improve social welfare. Raising taxes, on the other hand, removes purchasing power from the hands of people, and such moves are sometimes criticized on the grounds that they may seem to make people worse off than they were before the tax increase. If income taxes are increased, individuals or corporations have less cash available to spend, and this reduces excess demand and the pressure on prices. In the case of an increase in corporate taxes when inflation is pushing up costs, one hears that corporations are unable to bear this increase. And since investment funds are free to move wherever they seem most profitable, particularly if the funds originate from outside the country, then the levels of corporate taxation elsewhere become a very important consideration, for both investment and balance-of-payments reasons. Alternatively, the government may increase its commodity taxation as a means of reducing excess demand. That is to say, purchasing power is removed *as* the money is spent, rather than *before* it is spent as in the case of increases in income taxes. Because increases in commodity taxes raise the price of goods or services, some people mistakenly argue that this is a *cause* of inflation. Of course, this is not the case: if there is excess demand in the country, any increase in taxation, direct or indirect, will help to reduce inflationary pressures, so that the price pressure will likewise be reduced.

So the government's task is not an easy one. To fail to do the unpopular things is to be damned because inflation persists; to do them is to be damned because no one likes his taxes being raised. But the proper job of a responsible government is to do what is right even if it is sometimes unpopular, not to do just what is popular. And that is more easily said than done. One of the most important purposes of conferences of interested parties is to identify the issues, to clarify them, to discuss them, and to help develop a greater public understanding of the nature of the problem, the possible solutions, and the relationship between the interests of individuals or groups and that of the public at large.

Let me say a word about the task of reconciling economic goals. Stable prices are only one objective of government policy. The Economic Council of Canada has defined these others: full employment, a viable balance of payments, an adequate rate of economic growth, and an equitable distribution of rising incomes. If there are several objectives to be met, does this mean that some should be sacrificed so that others may be achieved? In recent years economists have been addressing themselves to the rather more sophisticated aspects of this question by asking not which objectives must be sacrificed, but rather what *combination* of sacrifices is necessary to give the best over-all performance? This, of course, is the familiar "trade-off." If we want no price increase whatsoever, how much unemployment will result? If we want full employment, how much will prices increase? And what is the best balance between these two objectives? There are many elaborations of these questions, involving the movement of prices in other countries, the position of our balance of payments, and the effects on different occupational classes in the country of varying rates of price increase, taking into account the creditor or debtor position of the various groups in the community, as well as the changes to be expected in income, employment, and production during inflationary periods.

Work in this area is important to policy-makers. If it seems evident from available data that inflation likely will set in before unemployment can be reduced by various policy measures to an acceptable level, then government measures clearly must be devised for the purpose of removing the bottlenecks which give rise to this problem.

Having said this, and I think the contribution of economic theory is very helpful in this regard, I think it is fair to suggest that this analysis is capable of misleading the uninitiated. There may be some who feel that the problem of reconciling goals implies a *conflict* of objectives, which must be decided in favour of one rather than the other. For example, if the study of trade-offs tells us that inflation has, in the past, set in when unemployment was still at an unacceptable level, some might argue that governments should concern themselves more about employment and sacrifice price stability to achieve higher levels of employment. I do not believe this to be the wisdom contained in these studies. I do not believe that full employment can be sustained with inflation, or that balance-of-payments problems can be neglected or solved by some easy gimmick, or that higher productivity comes automatically and can be achieved by some simple solution, such as ensuring full employment regardless of the inflationary consequences.

Rather, it is my firm belief that the major economic objectives of government must be worked out simultaneously and *can* only be achieved simultaneously. Attempts to neglect one aspect impede the achievement of others. Indeed, the major economic challenge facing Canada, the United States, and Western Europe is that of sustaining economic expansion without inflation. To my knowledge, this has never been achieved successfully before. Business expansions of varying length and intensity have always ended up in recessions or depressions, because they could not be sustained or perhaps because of bad management.

The fact that today Canada and the United States are in a period of expansion of record length offers hope, and also a challenge, to the policy-maker and to the people that it is possible to settle on and to follow a path of sustained growth without paying the heavy social and economic costs of a recession. In attempting to find this path of growth and how to get on it and stay on it, new instruments are being experimented with, discarded, improved upon, and sought for. Canada, I hope, is playing a positive role in this regard.

I should now like to make some rather more pointed observations about the Canadian economy. First, price increases this past year have clearly been greater than is healthy for the economy, quite apart from the hardship they work on people in our society whose bargaining power is relatively weak. Secondly, I believe the initial reason for these price increases was excess demand, and that this called for certain general measures on the part of government. Thirdly, I believe that some time during 1966 the psychological attitudes of Canadians about inflation, that is, how people by their actions responded to conditions, changed in such a way as to threaten to worsen the situation. Fourthly, I believe that the effects of government measures adopted, combined with a better degree of public understanding about the problem, have over the past few months reversed the psychological atmosphere and improved our prospects of returning to a more reasonable level of price stability in the period ahead. Fifthly, I believe that, to ensure relative price stability along with sustained economic growth, the best set of policies is a blend of general fiscal and monetary policies—measures which increase the productive capacity of the economy—combined with responsible behaviour on the part of all members of the community based on a clear appreciation and understanding of the nature of inflation.

Let me elaborate on each of these points. During 1966 the general price level of all goods and services increased by about 4 per cent over the preceding year, and consumer prices rose by something less than that. These increases are roughly double what they were in the preceding decade, a period which has been described as one of relative price stability. The main reason costs and prices rose more sharply last year was that we had reached a point of relatively full employment, and the total demands imposed upon the Canadian economy had grown to the point that they exceeded our ability to meet those demands. I shall say more about that in a moment. Before that, however, I want to say that I recognize there were special factors in 1966 which accounted for a good deal of the acceleration in prices. There were shortages of supplies of some foods, particularly meats, which led to higher food prices both here and in the United States. We are all aware that the increase in food costs has been under intensive scrutiny by a joint parliamentary committee. I think it is fair to say that, in general, there has been no main villain. In addition, prices have been rising more rapidly in the United States recently, and since many of the goods and services we use or sell are traded with the United States, this inevitably pushes up our prices.

Furthermore, the Canada and Quebec pension plans were introduced at the beginning of the year, added to payroll costs, and in an environment where these costs could be passed on much of this undoubtedly was reflected in higher prices. Another way of putting this, and I think not inaccurately, would be to say that Canadians demanded through their governments more social services and paid for them in part through higher prices.

Having recognized these special factors, I believe the main cause of our higher prices to have been excess demand. Our prices increased faster than those in the United States, where food prices also rose rapidly, and as fast as and in some cases faster than those of major European countries. Accordingly, the sharp improvement in our international competitive position which had been achieved over the past four or five years was brought to a halt; indeed, there may have been some small deterioration. This is a situation which obviously cannot long prevail, since it is clear that we can achieve higher levels of employment and rising levels of productivity only by increasing our trade with other countries, trade which has been growing most rapidly in the area of sophisticated manufactured goods.

Finally, despite the increases in prices which took place, the increase in costs to many businesses exceeded this, and corporate profits in total did not show much change in 1966 over 1965. I am aware of the proposition that profits rise very quickly in the earlier period of a business upswing and that wage incomes catch up in the later stages so that, according to this view, a profit squeeze is to be expected or even welcomed as a natural corrective. I am not going to try to judge whether any given level of profits is too high or too low—the market will do that, and investors will make the final decision about these things—but I do suggest to those who take an easy view about the "natural" swing away from profits in the latter stages of a business expansion, that the "natural" corrective for such a movement is a subsequent recession, which is precisely what we all want to avoid.

A few moments ago I referred to the demands being placed on

the Canadian economy in relation to our ability to meet those demands. Last year businessmen wanted to increase their investment by about 20 per cent, governments wanted to increase their spending rapidly, foreigners were placing great demands upon our resources through a rising and welcome increase in our exports, and finally, consumers wanted to improve even more rapidly their living standards and had the money income to try to do so. All of these demands were understandable, but they simply could not all be met at the same time.

Accordingly, the federal government took steps to attempt to reduce the increases in demand to something more in line with Canada's productive capacity. Some specific steps were taken in the autumn of 1965 to stretch out public capital expenditures, and the private sector was invited to follow suit. Then in the budget of March 1966 I introduced measures to stretch out business investment and to remove some of the excess purchasing power of individuals through restoring the personal income tax to its former higher levels, except for the lowest income earners. At the same time, the monetary authorities were following credit policies, with which I was in complete agreement, that were designed to hold the economic expansion to rates more in line with our underlying potential. The result was that continuing high levels of demand for credit pushed interest rates to very high levels, a trend that developed in the United States and Europe as well.

Meanwhile, the Government was continuing its efforts to develop programmes which would improve the mobility of our resources including, of course, trained labour, with the objective of increasing the supply of goods. It is too much to expect, of course, that shorter-run efforts at containing demand and longer-run measures for increasing production would immediately stabilize price levels in Canada. We recognized the effect of the lags in our economic system, the effect of outside forces, and the time involved for some of the programmes to be brought into effect. What we hoped to do was to contain or to reduce the rate of price increases.

I believe this combination of policies was beginning to work, but before the results could be seen, there occurred a change in the psychological attitude of many groups in the country. Some businessmen may have felt that the time had come to raise prices, rather

than try harder to reduce costs or to resist abnormal demands on
the part of labour. Others may have felt that the time had come to
get their share, or what they regarded as a fairer share, of the
growing national product by making wage demands, which taken
together were far in excess of what could be paid for out of the
growing productivity of the economy. At the same time, Parliament
and the provincial legislatures were authorizing a growing level of
government services. If this combination of attitudes or views had
continued to prevail, I believe the country would have faced very
serious difficulties. Those members of the community powerful
enough to achieve their objectives would have improved their
relative position, but only at the expense of the weaker ones. In the
end, we would have had a combination of still higher prices and
lower employment as a consequence of pricing ourselves out of
domestic and foreign markets. And the policy-maker would have
faced the dilemma some people see in the "trade-off" problem: To
offset the higher unemployment, brought about by too much demand, should *more* demand be placed on the economy, with the
result that prices would rise even faster?

In late 1966 the federal government tried to make quite clear to
the people of Canada the serious problems they confronted. We
pointed out that the general policies adopted to restrain inflation
were beginning to work but that responsible action and attitudes on
the part of the rest of the community were also necessary. We said
that we ourselves would not add to the inflationary pressures
through government actions. Accordingly, when the bill to provide
for supplementary payments to needy old age pensioners was
brought forward—a very desirable measure given the needs of so
many of these people on fixed incomes—I proposed a series of tax
measures designed to pay for the increased spending which would
result. In addition, we decided to postpone the introduction of
medicare for one year and undertook to reduce the rate of increase
in other worthwhile programmes.

We also considered other than fiscal and monetary measures. On
September 8 I said something about some of the newer experiments
in economic policy being attempted by various countries. I did not
propose any guideposts for specific prices or wage settlements, and
subsequently the Economic Council supported this decision. I did

point out as a matter of economic fact that, given our long-run productivity performance (which incidentally we have fallen short of in the past year or so) and given our price stability objectives, average money incomes per capita *could* not, as a fact of economic life, increase by more than 4 or 5 per cent a year. If some incomes were to increase more than that, then for a degree of relative stability to be achieved, this would involve others receiving increases less than that. I fully recognize the role of the market which requires that prices or wages move at different rates in order to bring about efficient transfers of resources. I also recognize that price stability does not mean price rigidity. But if, for economic reasons, some wages or prices go up more than average, and if stability is to be achieved, then others must expect lower than average increases. Indeed, I expressed the hope that some of the increases in productivity attained by some industries might be passed on to the consumer in the form of lower prices, rather than taken up by shareholders and workers. I also expressed hope that in time, through public discussion and understanding, voluntary actions taken by all groups in the country would be based upon a broader view of the effects of price and wage decisions.

In the latter months of 1966, I believe that, along with the effects of general fiscal and monetary policy, the climate of collective bargaining improved somewhat. Although increases in average earnings negotiated are still in excess of productivity gains, I believe and hope that we have passed through the worst period. At the time of heightened expectations in September, steel producers intended raising the price of this basic commodity. I considered that this would have aggravated the situation at the time and led to a worsening of the upward spiralling of wages and costs. Accordingly, I requested that the price increases be rescinded and the industry promptly complied. A few weeks ago, some steel prices were increased moderately, while other steel prices were reduced. I feel that the decision to hold back any price increase during the crucial period in the months following September was an important one.

While the current economic situation is by no means clear, it seems to me that the combination of policies I have described has begun to take hold. Increases in the consumer price index and in other measures of price performance are less now than they were six months ago, and at the very least I would think that in 1967 the rate of price increase will not accelerate. Indeed I would think that we can look for a slower rate of price increase in 1967. We cannot honestly expect to return immediately to the performance we achieved over the past decade because of the time lags involved in working through the economic system all of the things that have already taken place. The prospects for better price stability and sustained economic growth have, I think, been improved as a result of our policies. They have also been improved I believe by the shifting emphasis in the European countries and in the United States towards less restraint on the monetary side, brought about in turn by a better balance between fiscal and monetary policies.

In looking ahead to the future and based on the experience of the past, I believe that Canadian authorities, and that includes our provincial governments working out harmonious relations with the federal government, can improve upon our economic performance of the past. I believe this can be done through appropriate and well thought out fiscal and monetary policies, supplemented by policies designed to improve our supply capabilities and the general tone of the economy. Finally, as an additional new but important ingredient, we require the understanding and co-operation of the general public with respect to the individual decisions they make when they set prices or make wage demands.

In the Per Jacobsson Lecture he delivered at Rome last November, the Governor of the Bank of Canada said: "The experience of many countries suggests that monetary and fiscal policies need to be supported by some technique which mobilizes the force of public opinion behind non-inflationary behaviour by those who are in a position to deploy strong market power."

With that point of view, as a practising politician, I am inclined to agree. I am frank to add that I am not sure what the mechanism should be. Experience with guidelines, guideposts, incomes policies, and price and wage freezes in other countries does not inspire emulation. And yet there is undoubtedly some value in all of them in mobilizing and informing public opinion.

To be uncertain can be an asset. The nature of the Canadian economy is such that the policies of other countries—highly centralized or self-sufficient—should not be taken as necessarily applicable. Furthermore, what is called for is not a substitute for adequate general fiscal, monetary, trade, and productivity policies but a supplement to them. There cannot in the very nature of the problem be any simple mechanism applicable under all circumstances. After all, the aim is to influence public opinion and private behaviour, having in mind the broader national interest which is not always self-evident to individuals concerned with their immediate problems. This will require imagination and flexibility and at the same time a careful concern that public support develops for the new approaches to policy that may be developed.

A POLICY FOR CANADA

INTRODUCTION, *by John H. G. Crispo*

The stage has been well set for the final papers in this volume: Dr. Deutsch has put the whole question of wage-price-profit relations in its proper perspective; Professor Reuber and Mr. McQueen have admirably diagnosed the nature of the problems associated with these relations; Dr. Ross, Professor Smith, and the members of the recent OECD mission to Europe provided us with an insight into the way in which other countries are grappling with the same problems; and the Hon. Mitchell Sharp has analysed the situation as it appears in the eyes of the federal government. It remains for the authors of the following papers to provide us with "A Policy for Canada."

Let me put it this way. Either we do or do not have a significant trade-off problem, aggravated in small or large measure by the interaction of wages, prices, and profits. Some may feel there is no real problem, or at least none requiring major new departures in public policy. We would like to know why and how they reach this conclusion. We also wish to examine the point of view of those who think there is a problem requiring radical new alternatives, perhaps involving some kind of wage and price guidelines or incomes policies.

The ensuing discussions will provide varied answers to the questions raised in the previous papers.

A Policy for Canada

ARTHUR J. R. SMITH

I take my role to be that of presenting a summary of the policy conclusions and recommendations set forth in the Economic Council's *Third Annual Review*. Under this mandate, this summary will take the form, not of detailed etchings of various policy issues taken up by the Council, but rather of a broad-brush frescoe of the Council's main conclusions.

Such a summary will contain little that is novel. Yet, it can perhaps provide both a useful over-all framework and an appropriate point of departure for this panel discussion. Before attempting to outline the Council's policy position, however, I should emphasize that this position is based on certain very important premises. Four of these premises deserve special attention.

The first of these is that the goal of reasonable price stability is not one which is to be pursued in isolation, or one which is to be regarded as having priority above all others. This view conforms with the basic terms of reference in the act establishing the Council. The act makes clear that there are a number of basic economic and social goals to be achieved if the economy is to attain and maintain high standards of performance. Even the special reference to the Council on prices, costs, productivity, and incomes did not set price and cost stability as a pre-eminent goal; it explicitly mentioned a number of additional basic goals. In short, reasonable price stability is not a goal to be set on a pedestal above others, nor is it one to be achieved regardless of costs or consequences.

The second basic premise is that the market system is a fundamental feature of our economy and that prices have an important role to play in this system. Thus, price changes are not to be abhorred. They are, in fact, a normal and natural phenomenon in our system. But a satisfactory performance in regard to the goal of reasonable price stability requires that price increases should be largely offset by price declines within any broad measures of the over-all levels of prices. This view implies that the goal of reasonable price stability is not inconsistent with important changes in the structure of prices, changes which would help to point to those activities in which productive resources and services can make higher rates of return, and changes which help to provide signals for indicating what types of goods, what types of services, and what types of manpower are most in demand (or in short supply). By encouraging the reallocation of resources, the price mechanism contributes to the processes of change which lie deep at the heart of the whole process of economic growth. In this context, the Council's *Third Annual Review* favours the operation of effective market mechanisms:

We feel that for all their troubles and imperfections—for all the static and turbulence which they periodically generate—the essentials of the institutions of free collective bargaining and of flexible and relatively decentralized determination of wages and prices should be preserved. In the long run, they seem likely to be more compatible with good all-round performance by the Canadian economy than any visible alternative. However, in order to survive, they must continually demonstrate their ability to foster the processes of change and growth which are essential to the achievement of rising standards of living and to the development of a sound basis for the pursuit of other important economic and social goals (pp. 164–5).

A third basic premise is that there is *no policy for Canada* that can assure high standards of national performance if the international environment is unfavourable. No fact of Canadian economic life is more real or has more far-reaching implications for an understanding about the essential working of our economic system, than the fact that international economic conditions exert a powerful and pervasive influence throughout our economy. Not only do external conditions vitally affect, either directly or indirectly, almost every aspect of domestic economic developments, they also impose some important limitations on our freedom to use policies designed to mitigate unfavourable influences and to promote good performance in our economy. Thus, from the outset of its work, the

Economic Council has repeatedly emphasized that sustained and balanced growth of the Canadian economy close to its potential output path is simply not feasible against a background of output, employment, or price instability abroad, and especially in the United States.

The fourth basic premise may sound rather trite, but is no less important for that. It is that a good understanding of the *causes* of instability is essential to devising real solutions for its prevention or moderation. In short, policies must aim to deal with the underlying causes of problems, not with symptoms. This is especially important to emphasize in any discussion of price and cost instability. Inflation is a symptom of underlying pressures, distortions, and imbalances, and *effective* anti-inflationary policies must seek to correct these underlying problems.

It is a long leap from the Council's premises to its conclusions. But given the background which has been provided in many of the previous papers, I think I can immediately turn to a brief summation of these conclusions and recommendations. These can be grouped together under five principal headings: incomes policy, the "big levers" of demand policy, complementary supply policies, policies for special problem areas, and the development of more and better information, analysis, and public understanding about problems and policies.

The central conclusion in the area of incomes policy is a Council recommendation "against a formal incomes policy as a means of bringing about an improved reconciliation of high employment and reasonable price stability in Canada under normal peacetime conditions." In advising against the acquisition of this particular type of policy machinery, however, the Council stops short of outright rejection *under all circumstances*; a possibly useful, but temporary, role is indicated under emergency or crisis conditions, especially as a deliberate device to help "buy time" to put more basic corrective measures into effective operation. Perhaps neither supporters nor critics of this conclusion of the Council feel that the *Review* was as direct, or as neat and tidy, about the underlying reasons as it might have been. But it will be readily apparent that three sets of considerations helped to shape the Council's ultimate position on incomes policy.

The first set relates to the fact that foreign experiment and experience has not been highly encouraging in regard to the practical effectiveness of formal incomes policies to perform consistently well in relation to the principal goals they were designed to promote. In brief, incomes policies abroad appear generally to have promised more than they have in fact been able to deliver. In a number of cases they have apparently had some effect, but it is difficult to judge how great the effect has been, how long it has lasted, and whether in the end the initiative has been worthwhile.

A second set of reservations concerns some of the typical problems to which an incomes policy, by its very nature, gives rise: (*i*) the basic problem that, as a practical matter, such policies may introduce various rigidities which may adversely affect the processes of appropriate resource reallocation for growth; (*ii*) the problem that incomes policy assumes that the basic nature of cost and price increases reflects cost-push forces—perhaps largely emanating from the exercise of market power (as a consequence, if significant elements of demand inflation are at work, either a distorting repressed inflation may emerge, if the guidelines have some effect, or demand forces will break through the price and income guidelines in various places in disturbing ways); (*iii*) the practical difficulties of bringing appropriate national guidelines to bear in meaningful ways on individual price and wage decisions; (*iv*) the technical and other problems of devising appropriate guidelines figures to serve as a basis for such a policy; (*v*) the difficulties of devising and implementing adequate methods of persuasion to obtain compliance, unless there is both a willingness and a capacity to move, if necessary, towards significantly increased elements of control over prices and wages; and (*vi*) the problem which may turn out to be the most important of all, namely, that the struggle to operate an effective incomes policy may tend to divert energy and attention from other policies which could be more effective in the long run in helping to maintain reasonable price and cost stability.

The third set of considerations concerns factors bearing on an appropriate and effective use of such a policy in the Canadian environment. Even the most casual review of various foreign models of incomes policy suggests that none of these could be readily imported to Canada. Also, any careful review of foreign experience suggests that some of the problems encountered in their operation abroad might well be magnified under Canadian conditions. In its discussion of these considerations, the Council's analysis is based on the following question: "In what sort of country would an incomes policy have the best chance of success?" Canada does not appear to be a country providing a favourable environment by the criteria indicated by the Council. Among the considerations specifically cited in this context are: (*i*) the openness of the Canadian economy; (*ii*) the large degree of regional economic diversity; (*iii*) the wide decentralization of private decision-making and union and management organization; and (*iv*) the constitutional impediments to the development and use of government sanctions to maintain price and wage changes within a set of national guidelines.

Central to the Council's framework of positive recommendations is the view that the so-called "big levers" of demand-influencing policies—monetary and fiscal policies—must be "appropriately set" at all times. And central to the Council's view of the "appropriate setting" of these policies is the view that they should be essentially concerned with maintaining smooth and stable growth in *total final demand* close to the economy's growing *potential output*.

This basic strategy for operating the big levers is not new to the Council's *Third Annual Review*. It was articulated in general terms in the *First Annual Review* and further developed in the *Second Annual Review*. Taking account of the fact that both external conditions and internal instabilities may at times necessitate tactical departures from this basic strategy in the actual operations of these policies, the *Second Annual Review* outlined the appropriate roles of monetary and fiscal policies as follows:

Monetary Policy

We believe that the basic strategy of monetary policy should be concerned with expanding the money supply roughly in line with growing potential output, with a view to facilitating stable expansion of total final demand. We recognize, however, that the degree of success of such a monetary policy strategy will depend critically on whether a comparable strategy is being pursued in the United States. . . .

Short-term instabilities—of either external or domestic origin—are a prominent feature of sensitive financial markets. These may inevitably require tactical adjustments in monetary and debt management policies to meet special situations. . . .

Implicit in the above conclusion about the basic strategy for monetary policy is the view that monetary policy should not be essentially designed to deal with short-term cyclical instability in total demand. We believe that, within the limits which are necessarily imposed by external constraints, any fundamental adjustment in the basic strategy of monetary policy—that is, from the strategy of expanding the money supply roughly in line with potential output—should only be contemplated when final demand threatens either (1) to press in a persistent and prolonged way hard against the potential capacity of the economy to meet such demand, or (2) to fall persistently below potential, with a consequent prolonged situation of significant economic slack (p. 187).

Fiscal Policy
   We believe that the basic strategy of fiscal policy for stable growth [should involve] . . . a combination of levels of tax rates and expenditure programmes, taking all levels of government together, which would yield a rough balance on a national accounts basis (excluding the net accumulation of funds in the government-administered universal pension plans) if the economy were operating at potential output. This implies . . .
   —A deficit on this basis would automatically be generated when actual
      output is below potential output; conversely, under conditions of very
      strong demand, accompanied by shortages and bottlenecks leading to
      inflationary pressures, a surplus would also automatically emerge.
   . . . A basic adjustment of strategy towards greater restraint or towards greater stimulation, should depend on whether there are prospects for strong and persistent forces pressing the economy too rapidly or too hard against its potential or, conversely, prospects for the emergence of prolonged and significant economic slack (p. 188).

   In short, these views call for the formulation of these policies in relation to a longer perspective of economic developments and potentials than has typically been the case in the past. In part, this view rests upon the fact that long lags have generally occurred between short-cycle instabilities in the economy and the impact of changed policies to moderate such instabilities—sufficiently long lags to run serious risks that the policy changes might aggravate short-term cyclical instabilities rather than moderate them. Even if such lags could be reduced in the future, it is implicit in the Council's conclusions that the basic question which should motivate changes in those policies is not whether there is a current or impending business cycle contraction or expansion, but whether the economy may be faced with persistent and prolonged underutilization of its productive resources or whether it may threaten to press persistently against its capacity for reasonably full and efficient use of its resources. This focus will be especially important to keep clearly in mind over the next decade or more when an extremely high rate of growth in the labour force will make it necessary, for policy purposes, to appraise demand trends in the economy in relation to a very high, long-term rate of growth of both potential employment and potential output.

The *Third Annual Review* also helps to set these conceptions of the appropriate roles for the big levers into the context of its discussion of "trade-offs":

When actual output in the economy is falling persistently and substantially below potential output, with accompanying heavy unemployment and generally stable prices, it is clear that expansionary fiscal and monetary policies would be appropriate—and that it should be feasible to achieve a significant reduction in unemployment without encountering any significant degree of inflation. Conversely, when actual output is tending to press strongly and persistently against potential output (even though potential output is expanding), the general economic situation will almost invariably be one of very low unemployment and relatively strong general price advances. In these circumstances, it would be appropriate to deploy restraining fiscal and monetary policies—and it should be feasible to achieve a significant moderation of price and cost pressures without precipitating a substantial rise in unemployment. In short, the essential task of these so-called "big levers" of policy should be to try to keep the economy away from the upper and lower extremities of the trade-off zone (pp. 144–5).

An "appropriate setting" of the big levers, however, should be viewed as providing a necessary, but undoubtedly insufficient, condition for attaining and maintaining high standards of economic performance. Also needed is an important range of complementary supply policies and other special policies.

But before turning to these, I should mention two other important broad policies which have a very important bearing on the economy's performance. One is exchange policy; the other is commercial policy. As in the case of monetary and fiscal policy, an "appropriate setting" of both of these policies is a fundamental requirement. Both have far-reaching effects throughout the economy, and unless they are being properly operated, there is little that other policies can do to bring about a better reconciliation of our basic economic and social goals. The Council's position on exchange policy can be briefly summarized as follows:

We do not regard the present exchange value or any other exchange value of the Canadian dollar as sacred. Under the existing system, the exchange rate can be moved and ought to be moved when circumstances justify it. . . . The exchange rate should be treated neither as a national icon nor as an easy out, but rather as a potential policy option whose carefully considered use in proper circumstances can bring great benefit to an economy whose achievement of basic goals has in some way become seriously out of balance (p. 62).

The Council sees commercial policy not only as a useful means of exerting a pervasive resistance against rises in domestic prices of many goods relative to those abroad, but also as a means of encouraging competitively induced resource reallocation leading to improved longer-term growth in productivity and standards of living in Canada.

Complementing the role of the big levers for influencing total demand there is a need for a number of policies to work on the side of supply. There has been a growing recognition of the need for more effective policies of this type. But the heavy priorities in policy in the past have always tended to be on the demand rather than the supply policies. This is therefore a field which, according to the Council, needs to be given much greater emphasis and attention in the future. Here again, this is not a new theme in the *Third Annual Review*. It was also a key theme in the Council's first and second reviews.

It is recognized that many of these supply policies act even less quickly than the demand policies, and that they cannot be relied upon to provide any swift easing of pressures or distortions created by demand supply imbalances. But it is the Council's contention that the development and effective use of supply policies will help to moderate longer-run instabilities in the economy, while at the same time also working to improve, over the longer run, the reconciliation between the goals of high employment and reasonable price stability. Indeed, the Council has emphasized ever since the inception of its work that, in the light of postwar experience, the simultaneous achievement of the goals outlined in its *First Annual Review* would be extremely difficult, if not impossible, without more effective supply policies.

Among such supply policies, I would draw your attention particularly to those for improving productivity, for strengthening competitiveness, for facilitating adjustments to technological and other change, for dealing with pressure points and bottlenecks, and for increasing manpower training and mobility. In many ways, these are interrelated and interacting policies. For example, those which work towards improving competitiveness, such as policies designed to prevent the abuse of market power, will also tend to improve productivity. Those which facilitate adjustments to technological and other change will help to strengthen competitiveness. Those for increasing manpower training and mobility will help to facilitate adjustments to technological change.

Taken together, this whole range of policies may help to promote stronger and more stable long-term growth in total output and employment and thereby tend to ease the problems with which the general demand policies might otherwise have to cope. Moreover, unlike the general demand-influencing policies, many of these supply policies have a capability of being differentiated in their application between regions or between industries or sectors of the economy. They can therefore be concentrated on certain areas or sectors where they may be particularly effectively deployed to prevent various special kinds of strains or imbalances.

There are also other complementary policies needed to deal with certain special problem areas or to support the effective use of both general demand policies and the complementary supply policies outlined above. I will note only three of these policy areas which were covered by the Council.

The first concerns policies and planning (especially by governments) to achieve a smoother long-term growth of new construction expenditures. It was obviously not a new finding of the Council that *major* instability in the construction sector of the economy has been a *major* factor contributing to economic instability and to strong elements of price and cost pressures in the system. But the degree to which fluctuations in *government construction* expenditures have been a large aggravating factor in this instability was, I believe, both new and highly significant. Moreover, it is particularly the fluctuations in construction outlays under the control of the federal and provincial governments that have tended to accentuate this instability.

It was once believed, and still is believed in some quarters, that

governments could and should play an important stabilizing role in
the economy by increasing their investment activity when private
investment is weak and by moderating their investment activity
when private investment is exceptionally strong. What has generally
happened in the postwar period is that government investment has
tended to become weak when private investment is weak, and to
move up exceptionally rapidly when private investment is also
expanding rapidly.

The Council does not call for a policy of offsetting swings in
government investment to maintain more stable over-all investment
growth. It calls merely for an avoidance of fluctuations in government investment activity—particularly construction—that would
add to instability in private investment—in short, a smoother path
of long-term growth in government construction expenditures. This
requires, among other things, that governments take a long-term
view of their expenditure programmes (including, as the Council
had suggested in its two earlier reviews, the publication annually of
five-year capital budgets), better scheduling of construction expenditures in relation to the likely demand-supply situation of
the construction industry in key areas, more intergovernmental
co-ordination in this field, along with effective leadership by the
federal government both in the handling of its own construction
programmes and in whatever grants and shared-cost capital development programmes are undertaken with provinces and their
municipalities, and steps to bring about a greater centralization of
information and decision-making about construction expenditures
on the part of the federal government.

A second special area requiring improved policy formulation is
that of wage and salary determination in the government sector. In
this connection, the Council suggested a course of action for the
government:

The rapid expansion of the public sector together with the rapid development
of collective bargaining in that sector in recent years have considerably
enlarged the role of governments in wage settlements. These developments
make it mandatory that governments as employers become clearly aware of
the influence which wage decisions to which they are a party may have on
the economy, especially at a time of rising prices and costs. . . . It is impera-
tive that governments, and particularly the federal government, should

develop and adhere to certain basic principles and criteria relating to wage and salary policies and collective bargaining in the public sector (*Third Annual Review*, pp. 181–2).

The Council also suggested certain basic principles and criteria relating to this field of policy. The most important of these is that of maintaining as close a relationship as possible with wages, salaries, and other benefits paid by good employers in the private sector.

Third, the Council puts heavy emphasis on the need to move towards better co-ordinated federal-provincial fiscal planning. It does not suggest detailed ways in which this should be brought about, but it draws particular attention to the opportunities for improving intergovernmental liaison on economic matters through the regular meetings between federal and provincial finance ministers and treasurers towards the end of each calendar year. It suggests that the scope and importance of these annual meetings be enlarged, and that various documents should be published in advance of these annual meetings to provide the basis for broader debate, outside the meetings as well as within them, on general economic matters which must inevitably have an important bearing on decisions in the field of public finance. Among the specific proposals by the Council in this regard are: (*i*) to facilitate the lengthening of the time horizon in relation to which decisions should be made, the annual reviews of the Economic Council should be available in the autumn, along with a published survey of capital investment intentions for some years ahead, and (*ii*) publication in the autumn of an earlier version of the white paper on economics now published by the federal government shortly before its annual budget in the spring.

Finally, the Council has placed major emphasis on the need for better information, analysis, and public understanding about economic problems and policies: it called for a major strengthening of the Dominion Bureau of Statistics; it outlined a series of particular lines of economic research which it believes likely to yield useful ultimate results for policy purposes; it called for a better basis for a more informed public discussion and debate in the autumn of each year with the aid of some of the documents already noted above;

and it proposed that Parliament should consider setting up a standing committee on economic affairs of the Senate and the House of Commons, one of whose major purposes would be to conduct annual examinations of the above-mentioned documents and to hear expert witnesses on various aspects of economic problems and policies. It also emphasized that good decision-making—either private or public—depends crucially on good underlying information, analysis, and understanding about economic processes and relationships. And it recommends, in the interests of better public education and information about economic developments, that an independent institute of economic research should be established. The principal function of such an institute should be the publication of a regular bulletin containing analysis of shorter-term developments in the Canadian economy and the results of research on various economic problems and policy issues.

In this brief summary, I hope that I have been able to convey, in appropriate perspective, the wide range of issues taken up by the Council in its conclusions. If the total impression of my remarks is to convey that there are no simple or easy solutions to the problem of reconciling our basic national goals—and particularly of reconciling the goals of high employment and reasonable price stability—this will have conveyed an accurate view of the Council's position. As John Deutsch has emphasized in the first paper in this volume this basic problem of reconciliation has confronted every industrially advanced nation in the postwar period, and nowhere has there been discovered any easy remedies for it:

We have not any magic cure or simple formula to propose, but only a combination of tried and new approaches [which the Press has frequently misquoted as "tired and new approaches"] shaped as far as possible to what seem to be the significant peculiarities of the Canadian economy. Followed with energy, reasonable foresight, and consistency, in a favourable climate of public understanding, these approaches should be capable of gradually diminishing the problem. But spectacular, overnight results should not be expected of them. Particularly in such a field as price and cost behaviour, the sequence of premature expectations followed by disappointment and cynicism is especially to be avoided. Not only may it worsen the underlying situations; it may also lead to an unjustified early abandonment of the kind of sustained effort that is most likely to produce real improvement (p. 39).

Discussion

E. P. NEUFELD

J. L. FRYER

F. L. ROGERS

A. M. KRUGER

E. P. NEUFELD: It is my understanding that in this closing session we are to turn our attention to policy. What policy decisions should the nation take with respect to wage-price-profit relations? Perhaps the first one should be to banish the words "guidelines" and "incomes policies" from our language, for they have come to mean all things to everybody. Economists, including probably myself, are partially responsible for the confusion. Permit me to give you two pertinent examples. In his excellent survey study, *Incomes Policies*, prepared for the Economic Council of Canada, Professor David C. Smith very carefully recognizes the different meanings of these words. But he then goes on to choose one definition, he implies that it is *the* definition, and on that basis rejects an incomes policy in general. Specifically he says: "Better approaches may evolve, but instead of a comprehensive, official set of criteria or guidelines for individual wages and prices—which is the essence of an incomes policy—this alternative seems to be currently more suited to the Canadian economy." How different the tone of that definition from the one given by the Organization for Economic Co-operation and Development and reprinted in the *Third Annual Review* of the Economic Council of Canada: "What is meant by an incomes policy . . . is that the authorities should have a view about the evolution of incomes which is consistent with their economic objectives, and in particular with price stability; that they should seek to promote public agreement on the principles which should guide the growth of incomes; and that they should try to induce people voluntarily to follow this guidance" (p. 148).

My second example is taken from the *Third Annual Review* of the Economic Council of Canada. After concluding that "a formal incomes policy would not be an effective way of meeting the problem (of maintaining price stability) in Canada" (p. 190), the Council goes on to recommend that "governments should take immediate steps to improve the discharge of their responsibilities as major employers and increasingly large-scale direct participants in the process of collective bargaining. The object should be to develop sound criteria and principles and to avoid disturbing repercussions on the climate of collective bargaining in the private sector of the economy" (p. 192). Now forgive me if I lapse into a matter of semantics but I really do believe that the term "guidelines" might have been used in place of "criteria and principles." But then, you see, without having made any other change in the report, all the press would have reported that the Council *favoured* guidelines, instead of the opposite.

Before outlining my own views about desirable policy action I would like to state, without argument, some of the major points that seem to me to be important:

(1) The major cyclical distortions that must be dealt with by policy-makers are the volatility of capital spending and inventory accumulation, and the tendency for excessive profit increases and excessive wage increases to appear in sequence over the cycle.

(2) It may be that if the former problem is solved, the latter will be less serious than it has been.

(3) The steps taken in the budget of March 1966 were an important beginning in experimenting with techniques designed specifically to control the volatility of capital spending in the private sector. Further experimentation will undoubtedly be necessary, and some progress must be made in bringing increased stability to the public sector.

(4) Because of the possibility that steps such as these will reduce the cyclical distortions in wage/profit income distribution, and because of the undesirable impact detailed controls might have on the ability of the economy to allocate labour and materials in an

efficient way, I would reject Professor Smith's concept of an incomes policy as a basis for action—just as he rejected it.

(5) However my view is that some experimental action should nonetheless be taken, for these reasons:

(*i*) It is unlikely that excessive cyclical instability in capital spending will be entirely removed in the near future.

(*ii*) It is not at all certain that even if it were, the tendency for profit/wage relationships to become distorted would then disappear.

(*iii*) Economists are unlikely to reach a consensus as to the precise nature of the profit-wage-price relationship, so experimentation with techniques seems a good place to start.

(*iv*) The management and labour-union power blocks in some areas will likely continue to exercise monopoly influences on the price of labour and the price of goods and services.

(*v*) The resolution of the management/labour conflict through collective bargaining may not in itself in all cases produce economically desirable results for the nation, but even more so, any tendency for compulsory arbitration to be used more frequently would make it absolutely essential for the arbitrators to have the best possible guidelines.

(*vi*) The government is already deeply involved in settling wage disputes and in such cases the process of collective bargaining seems to me to be seriously compromised, perhaps even conceptually irrelevant. Again, some kind of guidelines would seem to be called for immediately in such cases.

For all these reasons I favour some action relating to wages, prices and profits. But what kind of action?

(1) I agree with Professor Smith and the Economic Council that steps should be taken to increase our knowledge of these matters and to achieve improved public understanding of the issues. I disagree most strongly with their view that this should be done by establishing a new independent research organization, for two reasons. First, there is no assurance at all that without explicit instructions and responsibilities such an independent organization would provide the continuing and regular flow of information on badly needed short-term developments. Second, it is the kind of work that the Economic Council should be doing, for several reasons:

(*i*) The apparent belief in the Council, and certainly one embodied in its terms of reference, that it can successfully and to good effect concentrate on medium- and long-term economic developments without a close and continuing appraisal of short-term developments is, in my view, quite mistaken. The very fact that the Economic Council in its annual reviews fairly frequently dips its toe, however gingerly, into the hot and turbulent waters of short-term developments is an indication of the conceptual nonsense in its terms of reference. The Council's work would be improved if it forthrightly admitted the importance of the short-run for its work. If this required a change in its term of reference, so be it; it would be easier than establishing another research body.

(*ii*) The supply of good economists is scarce, thus the need to avoid unnecessary duplication is very pressing indeed.

(*iii*) The Council has already developed public relations procedures that are useful for general educational purposes.

(*iv*) If it were thought that it would be "politically" difficult for the diverse Council members to endorse a report discussing the hot issues of current developments, a solution might be to simply permit a section of the Council to produce a report on short-term developments without any endorsement by Council members, as is done with the special studies.

In short, I strongly recommend that the Economic Council of Canada be given the responsibility for engaging in on-going research in the specific area of profit-wage-price developments, and in short-term economic developments in general, and in a way that improves the public's understanding of the issues.

(2) Apart from basic research on the nature of the profit-wage-price relationship, in what kind of general activities relevant to the subject matter of this Conference should the Council be engaged?

(*i*) It should bring public opinion closer to the price-setting developments in industries by compiling and publishing statistics and charts of price changes in a great range of industry and sub-industry groups and analysing those changes.

(*ii*) It should annually indicate what, to the best of its knowledge and within the context of an economic forecast, it would regard as economically acceptable increases in general wages and prices.

(*iii*) It should critically examine major wage increases of the preceding year and pricing policies of individual industries over that same period, as well as wage-profit relationships.

(3) Then there is the problem of defining "criteria and principles," for wage settlements involving the Government of Canada in a fairly direct way, and in cases where a dispute has gone to compulsory arbitration. Can anyone possibly argue that the best possible guidelines based on economic criteria, however inadequate, should not be made available in such cases? Vague generalizations and moralistic exhortation simply are not good enough.

This then is the over-all approach I would recommend. I cannot understand why there should be any delay in implementing it.

JOHN L. FRYER: I shall not be able to provide a thorough investigation of the very complex economic relationships and policy implications inherent in any discussion of whether or not full employment is compatible with price stability and if so by which methods such a highly desirable state of economic affairs should be achieved. The best I can do is make some rather subjective comments on certain aspects of the debate that seem to me to require particular attention.

The debate is not a new one for writing on the same subject more than twenty years ago, Lord Beveridge saw the need for price controls together with a more responsible system of collective bargaining as part of any programme designed to assist the process of reconciliation. The task of achieving compatibility remains unfinished; yet its solution is hardly facilitated by what I feel is an observable propensity on the part of successive Canadian governments to place an extraordinarily high priority on the goal of price stability. Furthermore, the level of much recent economic discussion in this country has hardly been enhanced by a preoccupation, on the part of far too many people, with the real and imagined dangers of real and imagined inflation. A correspondent for *The Economist* expressed this concern far better than I when he wrote:

More cant is mouthed about inflation than almost any other subject in the economic lexicon. Governments vow to abolish it (and they don't). The legion of the wise warn that nations will wilt under it (and they don't). So instead of pretending that inflation will be ended, and must be, it's more sensible to recognize that stamping out the last two percent of inflation is usually more trouble than it's worth.[1]

Recently the cries of alarm have subsided as many observers have become acutely conscious of the very delicate balance of our economy in centennial year. In our view there was a great deal more concern about inflation in 1966 than the conditions actually warranted. We were worried, and still are, that if the government is pressured into taking major restraining action on the economy— particularly in the form of large cutbacks in government spending— the result could well be to damage the growth potential of our economy and to create a high-unemployment situation.

We were therefore particularly gratified to see the well-reasoned treatment of the subject of prices, costs, incomes, and productivity and their relationship to sustained economic growth contained in the *Third Annual Review* of the Economic Council of Canada. This examination, emanating from the request for such a study transmitted to the Economic Council by the Government in 1965, is a valuable addition to the body of available economic knowledge in this country. In their study of the relationship between the level of employment and the achievement of price stability, the Council dealt at some length with the subject of incomes policies and their appropriateness to the Canadian scene.

In considering policies for price stability the Council rejected a formal incomes policy, except possibly under rare emergency conditions, and then only on a temporary basis. They interestingly emphasize that this finding applies only to the kind of incomes policy that is concerned with achieving price stability at high levels of employment. It does not apply to a wide variety of taxation, welfare, and other policies that have a bearing on the distribution of income. Thus defined, the Council makes a compelling argument that the obstacles in the way of incomes policy in Canada—our federal structure, the relatively unorganized state of both labour and management, and the difficulty of enforcing decisions—will remain insurmountable in the foreseeable future and may also serve to detract attention from more immediate policy considerations.

The distinction between different types of incomes policies made

[1]*The Economist*, October 8, 1966, 169.

by the Council in its third review is extremely important especially when the attitudes of various sectors in the economy towards such policies are being assessed. In our view there is an urgent need for a more egalitarian distribution of our nation's wealth. It is unfortunate, therefore, that all too often incomes policy appears to have become a euphemism for wage policy and this, in turn, has been used as synonymous with wage restraint. If labour has not been noticeably enthusiastic about incomes policy the reason lies here. On the other hand, labour would certainly give consideration to, and be prepared to discuss with other groups, an incomes policy that formed part of a total plan to distribute our nation's economic wealth more equitably.

In rejecting a formal incomes policy as the best method of reconciling the apparently dichotomous goals of full employment and reasonable price stability, the Council reiterated its contention that these goals could best be achieved through a more intelligent and more effectively planned use of fiscal and monetary policies. They criticized governments for having used these "levers" inappropriately in the past and for having been too concerned with minor short-term fluctuations in the economy. The simultaneous achievement of price stability and balanced income distribution in an economy approaching full employment is a formidable economic task if indeed it is attainable at all.

In concluding I would venture to suggest that perhaps the time has come when Canadians and those charged with the responsibility of managing our economy should recognize and accept the following facts of economic life:

(1) Price stability is only one of a number of desirable economic objectives, and not necessarily the chief one.

(2) Some upward creep in prices is probably unavoidable as we move closer to full employment.

(3) A moderate price rise is really a small price to pay for the enormous social and economic benefits of full employment and rapid economic growth.

(4) Given our enormous productive capacity, we are extremely unlikely to suffer an uncontrollable inflation in the absence of a major war.

(5) In any case, we can, if we have the courage and imagination,

minimize the trade-off between inflation and unemployment by modifying a number of "expendable" practices which give an upward bias to the general price level and by developing new arrangements and new institutions which make the economy less inflation-prone at high levels of employment.[2]

FORREST L. ROGERS: Rather than attempting to range quickly over the basic policy issues that others would no doubt be dealing with, I decided it would be much more useful to present some of the critical reactions I have had to the work of the Economic Council. Not all of these criticisms relate specifically to the area of wage-price problems, but all of them, I believe, have relevance to the objective of securing continued improvements in the formulation and activation of economic policies in this country. First, then, may I suggest that the Council, after explicitly interpreting its basic mandate as being to investigate and report upon the medium- and long-term prospects and problems of the Canadian economy, has in certain important respects failed to do what could legitimately be expected in this regard. I do not, of course, refer to the excellent work done in the area of supply considerations and touching on manpower utilization, education, productivity, and so on. But what I do have in mind is that, after setting out a very helpful pattern of objectives and other considerations relating to the growth of the Canadian economy from 1963 to 1970 in its first report, the Council has in its two subsequent reports provided only the briefest and most superficial of attention to the question of how one should reassess its first projection for the balance of the sixties in the light of actual developments to date. To cite only one example, which relates directly to the area of wages and prices, the latest report contains only the most general of references to the question of what has been happening to Canada's international competitive position as a result of the wage and price trends of the past two years. There is some discussion, of course, of relative price trends in various countries, but there is no serious attempt at all to relate these to either recent or prospective trends in international payments.

[2]Irv Beller, "The Guideposts: Objections and Alternatives," *George Washington Law Review*, vol. 35, no. 2, December 1966, 274–85.

My second point of criticism, which is closely related to the first one, is that after saying that its basic concern is with medium- and longer-term matters and officially eschewing any responsibility for assessing short-term conditions, the Council in fact has not been able to refrain from analysing and commenting upon these conditions in such a way as to carry unmistakable implications with respect to current policy issues. The temptations to perform in this way are, of course, understandable to any government or business economist, but the result of the Council's ambivalent posture towards these matters has been that its reports have not included specific or adequate references to many of the significant elements in the near-term outlook that decision-makers simply have to take into account. Nevertheless, despite the partial and strained character of the Council's discussions pertaining to current policy issues, the press and others have picked up what the Council has had to say and thereby registered the weight of its prestige on particular sides of the issues concerned. From the standpoint both of good decision-making and of public understanding of what is involved, I believe that this situation is far from satisfactory.

Because the Council has seemed to place itself in a kind of privileged arms-length position in relation to the "bear-pit" of current economic policy debate, I believe it is appropriate to inject a personal judgment that the Council, in what description it has presented of recent business trends, has clung much too rigidly to the stereotyped kind of cyclical analysis which has had so much technical elaboration during the postwar years. Without denying the value of the technical advances that have been made in this direction, I believe that the Council has seriously underplayed the non-cyclical influences flowing out of the Vietnam war in each of its last two reports, and on reflection suspect that this is just one major example of a general tendency in the Council's work. On reflection, also, I have wondered whether this apparent inflexibility of analytic approach might not somehow be related to the position the Council has taken with respect to its official role in the policy sphere.

The next question I would like to raise, and one that comes more to the heart of the issues of current concern, has to do with what I believe has been an unduly expansionist bias in the Council's presentations to date. This bias was neither too apparent nor in any case too objectionable in the Council's first annual report, having regard for the continued existence of unutilized productive resources and for the large prospective increase in the labour force, which the Council delineated so well. There was good reason, however, to question the wisdom of the 3 per cent unemployment target which the Council approved in that first report—or perhaps more accurately it should be said that there was reason to question the failure of the Council to impress upon the public the significance of the long-run structural changes that were required to make the target consistent with other basic objectives. Following upon this initial weakness, the Council in its second report, released in December 1965 was plainly caught short by the swift upsurge of demands that was stimulated by the step-up of military activity in Vietnam. Had the Government taken account only of the Council's implied policy recommendations in that report, we might well have let ourselves in for even more inflationary problems than we have in fact encountered in the past year. I believe the same expansionary bias is apparent in the third report. In part, I hinge this judgment on the inadequate attention paid to the range of possible developments with respect to Vietnam; here it may well turn out that the Council's complacency in this respect is quite appropriate, if in fact the lower estimates of US defence costs and the related softening in US business trends do hold sway. At the same time, I believe that in the light of the trends over the past few years, there is a real question as to whether it is desirable or not to maintain a consistently one-sided view of aggregate demand prospects for the medium term.

I suppose further evidence of expansionary bias is the Council's expression of such grave doubts about the value of a discretionary fiscal policy (in its second report) and of wage-price guidelines (in its third report). In both instances, a key argument in favour of the respective policies was to impose some restraint upon undue wage-price pressures in the economy. Thus, in the immediate context at least, opposition to the use of such policies could be said to reflect a greater interest in expansion for its own sake than in the other objectives of reasonable price stability and balance-of-payments equilibrium. Whether this is a valid point or not, I do believe that the Council has taken an unnecessarily defeatist stand on both of these important policy questions. Fortunately, the Government was not swayed by the Council's negative views of early 1966 about discretionary fiscal policy; indeed, one of the most encouraging aspects of policy development over the past year is the progress that has been made in introducing much-needed flexibility into the operation of fiscal policy as economic conditions evolve and change.

With respect to wage-price guidelines, I cannot in this paper comment adequately on what is probably one of the most burning individual policy issues confronting this country. However, I do want to indicate clearly that my position is in whole-hearted agreement with the views of the many American and Canadian students of the issue who see the development and administration of such guidelines as a significant supplementary tool of economic policy in the modern North American economy. Successful results from guidelines will be greatly dependent upon the wise adjustment of the "big levers" of fiscal and monetary policy, but contrary to what the Economic Council implies, I do not believe that you have to have perfection in all of these spheres in order to get useful results. The perfect should not be allowed to become the enemy of the good. My own conviction is that pursuit of a pragmatic and judicious guidelines policy will produce not only a worth-while improvement in economic policy results, but also a much-needed spread of public understanding about what is most in the national economic interest at particular times. I hope you will note, also, that in these all-too-brief comments I have talked in terms of wage-price guidelines and not in terms of some sort of more comprehensive incomes policy. In terms of what appears practical and useful in the current North American context, it is only the question of guidelines and not something broader and more diffuse that requires serious thought and debate.

There is now one further brief criticism of Council presentations that I wish to make, before seeking to justify the whole series of criticisms by drawing from them at least a few positive suggestions that are worthy of further discussion. This last point of criticism is that all of the Council's references to monetary policy thus far fall far short of the modern standards of discussion that have been established in this country by the Bank of Canada and all of the work associated with the Royal Commission on Banking and Finance. Beyond this, I found it almost unbelievable that the

Council could, in its *Third Annual Review*, set out a proposed schedule for formal analysis and discussion of official economic policies without any reference at all to the Bank of Canada. In fact, for all of the traditional reticence of central banks to express views about economic conditions ahead or to get too close to the specifics of fiscal policy, the Bank of Canada has provided some of the most helpful light on the nature of our main policy problems that has been available in the past two or three years.

Now to draw upon my list of critical comments in order to suggest helpful improvements in our ability to cope with wage-price and profit problems in the years ahead, I would suggest first that we have reached the stage where we need to carry out a careful re-assessment of our present organizational approach to the formulation of economic policies in general and to coping with wage-price problems in particular. In this regard, I believe that the Economic Council contributed a key constructive suggestion when it recommended the establishment of a standing parliamentary committee, with adequate research assistance, as the focus for public discussion of economic policy issues. Beyond this, however, I think there is great need for a more realistic appraisal of how the schedule of analytic responsibilities and of reports should be organized and in particular of the Council's own role in the process. The question of timing is also important, for as we have seen in the past year or so, analyses prepared at particular times have been seriously out-paced by the course of events, and in addition the need for greater flexibility than has been traditionally embodied in annual federal and provincial budgets has become patently clear.

To make use of the standing committee idea, I believe it would be necessary to work out a once-a-year schedule of reports and discussion focused particularly on the over-all shape of federal and provincial budgets. Perhaps it would be necessary to concentrate this process in the autumn months, as the Council suggests, even though the actual budgets are presented in March or April. If this is so, there should at least be provision for a quick review of the discussions just prior to March and April to see if previous views still hold. It would be desirable also formally to envisage occasional adjustment of the fiscal levers as a normal possibility during the course of a year. Beyond this, of course, there is the question of what reports should be presented before the standing committee and what content should be expected in them. Here I would suggest that reports be expected from government departments, from the Bank of Canada, and from various private organizations and individuals, all focusing upon the short-run adjusting of the fiscal and monetary levers. Perhaps, also, provincial representatives could take part in this process, along with continuing their direct discussions with the federal government.

There remains the awkward question of how the Economic Council itself should fit in. And this, as should be clear by now, is the primary question with which I have been concerned in this whole presentation. The Council, I believe, did a good job in its first projection of longer-term considerations affecting the Canadian economy, and it has done good work also in its investigations of various supply problems, particularly centring on the question of productivity improvement. By reason of its organizational structure, which is based on the representation of specific interest groups in the economy, one would expect the Council to be most useful in dealing with problems which particularly require a melding of these differing points of view. Thus, the study of ways to improve productivity seems entirely appropriate. I feel also that the Council in its present form is well-suited to play an important role in the formulation and perhaps even the administration of wage-price guidelines, although final responsibility would have to rest with the government of the day. On the other side of the picture, I feel that the Council as presently organized is not particularly well suited to play a primary role in the shorter-run economic analysis and discussion designed to assist in the development of general fiscal and monetary policies, and I am not even sure that it is the best kind of body to carry out the longer-run studies aimed to provide adequate perspective in this policy process. We undoubtedly need to give more thought to just what sort of longer-term analysis should be encouraged and what is the best way to carry it out. Meanwhile, we already have a number of people, in both public and private positions, who are working regularly in the area of shorter-run analysis, and the Council has suggested a system centring around a standing parliamentary committee, which could provide a needed focus for more effective public discussion of the economic policies required.

It seems to me, therefore, that it should not be very difficult to get a more satisfactory organization of our efforts to achieve better policy performance, and that improvement in this direction may well be as important in the long run as the studies carried out on the policy problems themselves.

ARTHUR M. KRUGER: We have been asked to begin by indicating whether or not we believe in the "Philips' curve," or in the notion that policy-makers must accept more rapid price increases when the unemployment rate falls, and more unemployment when the rate of price rise is reduced. I do believe that the existence of such a "trade-off" has been established. However, I am not happy with the way the question has been posed. The economic goals of our society include targets in areas other than inflation and unemployment. Policy must be viewed in this multi-dimensional perspective rather than in the limited framework of the unemployment-inflation trade-off. The Economic Council of Canada has listed rapid economic growth, a viable balance of payments, and an equitable distribution of incomes in addition to full employment and reasonable price stability as the key goals for Canada. To this list I would add the goal of maintaining the private decentralized decision-making system as the central mechanism for determining the allocation of our economic resources and the composition of our output of goods and services. While the Council's reports implicitly support this objective, they fail to list it as a central goal of economic and social policy.

Once we recognize the multiplicity of policy goals, then we see that even if the guidelines or some other programme worked, in that it enabled us to reduce unemployment and inflationary pressures simultaneously, this would not necessarily be a blessing. We might reject such a programme because of its cost in the sacrifice of one or more of the other policy objectives.

The least objectionable sort of guidelines policy in terms of these other objectives is the pure "jawbones" version: the government refrains from exercising coercion and limits its role to urging labour and management to act with restraint in setting wage rates and prices. The idea is that if the *average* rate of wage increase is kept to the level of aggregate productivity gain, and if the average level of profits is maintained, then some prices will rise (in sectors where productivity gains are sluggish) and others will fall (in sectors where productivity rises rapidly), so that on balance the price level remains fairly stable.

This approach raises the serious problem of devising adequate statistical measures of productivity and also introduces the questionable assumption of the equity of existing relative shares received by labour and management and the distribution of payment within labour and management. It acknowledges the necessity and even the desirability of permitting substantial deviation in particular wages and prices from the norm, thus providing little in the way of real guidance in any particular situation. Finally, it asks the parties to forego voluntarily some of the material benefits they could attain in the interest of price stability. If our collective-bargaining or product-pricing system were highly centralized, one might hold out the hope that such an appeal could work. The parties might then see that a higher wage or price than that set by the guidelines would soon be eroded by inflation. In such a system, the parties would realize that what counted was their "real" gains, not the illusive monetary gains that accompany inflation. But neither our wage-setting nor our price-setting arrangements are so centralized. In any given situation it is impractical to expect the parties to see that voluntary restraint will pay off by suppressing inflationary pressures or that "excessive" wage or price changes will be eroded by inflation. In no single wage or price-setting unit in Canada will it be found beneficial to withhold the full exercise of market power in order to curb inflation. In most cases, the parties fail to see any inflationary effects of their actions. Even where this is visible, they feel that on balance they still benefit by maximizing monetary gains, since they have little confidence that other price-setters will exercise similar restraint.

The jawbone attack is doomed to fail in a system of private decentralized price and wage setting, where decisions are based on the desire of the decision-makers to maximize their material well-being. The notion of voluntary restraint runs directly counter to the pursuit of self-interest so pervasive in our sort of system and so vital to the preservation of this system which most of us feel is worth preserving.

If the guidelines policy will not work where freedom to set wage rates prevails, let us consider Professor Neufeld's suggestion concerning its value in those sectors of the economy subject to intensive government intervention perhaps even in the form of compulsory arbitration. First, let me say that compulsory arbitration, in my opinion, should be limited to those disputes where a work stoppage would create a serious threat to the health and safety of a large section of the population. I would oppose using compulsory arbitration, either generally or in selected sectors, as a device to suppress inflationary pressures except under severe crisis conditions such as those occurring during a war. If arbitration is limited to sectors where a work stoppage would be intolerable, then the arbitrators must seek to impose a settlement which the parties feel is acceptable, rather than follow guidelines designed for other purposes. It would be both unfair and impractical to expect policemen, firemen, and other workers in similar critical sectors to abide by the wage guidelines, while workers elsewhere could strike for much higher settlements. In any case, if we agree that arbitration should be confined to a small number of cases, the impact on over-all prices and wages would be negligible even if arbitrators could manage to impose a guideline on wage rates in these few sectors.

An alternative suggestion for improving the terms of the trade-off between our employment and price objectives involves the use of manpower and other programmes designed to promote the mobility of labour (and other resources) so as to ease the "bottlenecks" which are held responsible, in part at least, for the rise in wages and in other prices, while unemployment and idle capacity in other resources persist. This approach has the blessing of the Economic Council and provides the basis for the creation of the Department of Manpower. However, I am troubled by the speed with which we have embraced this new panacea. Here, I cannot do more than indicate the basis for my concern.

One of the arguments cited in favour of an active manpower policy is that inflationary pressure is generated by the sluggish adaptation of factor allocation, particularly labour, to changes in demand. Also, such lags are said to retard economic growth. The policies are supposed to go beyond correcting past and current deficiencies and to anticipate future market changes.

How does one identify a true "bottleneck"? If employers contend that they cannot get sufficient labour at the wage rates currently offered, does this justify state action to assist them? Why should they not be asked to follow the normal practice of offering higher wage rates to attract workers or of substituting other factors for the scarce kinds of labour? In helping employers who face labour "shortages," we may be subsidizing firms whose wage rates have lagged either because they have been slow to respond to market pressures or because their very existence may no longer be justified. In channelling workers to specific sectors or regions, we are not only influencing manpower allocation, but also altering relative factor prices, the methods of production which firms use, the relative prices of goods and services, and the composition of our national product. These side effects of manpower policies tend to be ignored by the proponents of manpower programmes. Nonetheless, the adverse impact on consumer sovereignty of such programmes is very real. Further, these policies *may* retard long-run economic growth even where some short-run gains in output can be demonstrated.

Where manpower programmes are addressed to anticipated changes in labour demand, the policies must rest on forecasts of expected change. I am very hesitant to suggest that education, training, worker relocation, immigration, or other important programmes should be based on the results of the sort of forecasts which economists are able to generate. Such forecasts rest on a host of assumptions concerning future technological change, consumer tastes, government policies, events abroad, and so on, all of which rest on the judgment or hunches of the forecaster, rather than on any scientific basis. The most interesting kinds of manpower programmes, those addressed to future changes, suffer both from their dependence on forecasts and from their unanticipated and perhaps dysfunctional influence on the composition of product output, the allocation of resources, and the speed and direction of technological change.

I have concentrated thus far on criticizing the policy proposals of others. Now I want to put forward several suggestions of my own, none of which are original or dramatic. These proposals, I feel, are consistent with our desire to balance off the various policy goals enumerated earlier.

My first suggestion is a gradual reduction of all tariffs so that we can benefit from foreign competition. This would serve not only to lower prices in Canada, but also to promote more rapid economic growth here by inducing a shift in our resources to areas where our comparative advantage is greatest. If such tariff reduction could be part of a reciprocal arrangement with other countries, all the better. However, if no such deals can be worked out, we would benefit nonetheless from unilateral action.

Next I suggest the need for a complete overhaul of our anti-combines legislation and enforcement procedures. There is no need to wait for the industry studies which the Economic Council intends to undertake. The weaknesses of our legislation are well known as is the need for a larger budget for those entrusted with the investigation and prosecution of combines. Vigorous action to generate competition in product markets would serve to lower prices directly. It would also inhibit union ability to raise wages and so further contribute to controlling prices.

Finally, there are numerous examples of existing public policies that serve to promote collusion and economic gains for the producers of certain goods and services at the expense of the public. We should re-examine the basis for limited licensing, the rigid, lengthy educational qualifications for admission to trades and professions, the impact of state marketing boards for farm products, and other policies which often limit competition and keep prices above the competitive level.

We seem to have a low tolerance for the discomforts which accompany either unemployment or inflation. Our first reaction is to summon the "doctor" and to urge the state to prescribe as drastic a medicine as may be necessary to curb whichever of these afflictions may be troubling us most at the moment. The "trade-off" indicates that in combating one social illness we unfortunately aggravate the other. The prescribers of policy then seek ways of coping with both problems simultaneously through guidelines or manpower programmes. Weak injections seem to be ineffective while strong effective doses generate such severe side-effects as to raise doubts about the efficacy of the prescriptions. My own feeling is that we should limit intervention to the tried and proven monetary and fiscal remedies supplemented by action designed to permit the system to purge itself through the operation of the market mechanism.

We should refrain from panic each time either unemployment or, more particularly, inflationary pressures rise above some "critical" level. Frankly, at no time in the postwar period have these problems got so far out of hand that drastic remedies were called for. We have managed to move along the trade-off curve over a range where neither unemployment nor inflation has reached really serious levels. We have achieved this with monetary and fiscal policies and with little sacrifice to our other social objectives. While we should always seek to do better, there is no justification for panic.

Perhaps what I am really suggesting is that there is no urgent wage price employment problem which requires massive attention or action. The undue emphasis given to this subject has tended to obscure other more pressing areas, such as the environment in our cities or the plight of the family, where research and public action are urgently needed.

Conference Summary

JOHN H. G. CRISPO

It remains for me to endeavour to summarize the views which have been expressed in these various presentations on "Wages, Prices, Profits, and Economic Policy." It would be presumptuous of me to suggest that they represent a consensus. It would be difficult enough to do justice to the last few papers let alone all of them. However, perhaps I may be permitted a few observations embodying some of the thoughts I have derived from them.

It seems to me that there is broad agreement that Canada does face a trade-off problem between full employment, stable prices, and certain other desirable economic and social objectives, although there is variation in the assessment of the magnitude of the problem, largely because of the different priorities of the authors. If I may refer solely to the choice that appears to have to be made between full employment and stable prices, it is clear that some are more inclined to favour the pursuit of full employment at the expense of price stability, while others have the opposite preference.

Second, while there is agreement that there is a trade-off problem, there does not seem to be agreement on the extent to which it is caused by the interaction of the competing economic groups represented in the wage-price-profit relationship. Indeed, I have the impression that union and management have arrived at a kind of *quid pro quo* in this area, with neither willing to make too much of an issue of the other's activities so long as this attitude is reciprocated by the other. If I were a cynic, I might even go further and state that their mutual desire to convince others that the wage-price-profit relationship is not a major contributing factor reflects the joint vested interest which organized advantaged groups have in taking advantage of disorganized disadvantaged groups.

Third, as to what should be done about the trade-off problem, a range of opinions has been expressed, particularly on the question of wage and price guidelines and incomes policies, but there is an obvious split on the issue. For myself, I would note that while I still experience from time to time a heady emotional desire for some kind of wage and price guidelines and incomes policies—for the sake of equity if nothing else—my economics background and my knowledge of the practical realities of industrial relations life constantly bring me back to earth. Even the mildest forms of wage and price guidelines or incomes policies disturb me, because once a society starts down this pristine garden path it may find it extremely difficult to reverse itself. The experience of several countries suggests that once that fateful first step is taken, it is regrettably easy to move towards even more stringent forms of regulation and control.

Fourth, I think there was agreement that even if we move in the direction of a guidelines or incomes approach, this would not by itself solve the problem. That many other programmes are required, especially in the manpower field, has been made clear by many of the contributors. These policies are required both on the demand and the supply side of the market and together entail an arsenal of public policies designed to reduce the unpleasantness of choosing between full employment and stable prices.

Finally, I hope there was agreement that under no circumstances should we panic and rush ahead and adopt some foreign innovation which may or may not work in its own home environment let alone in a different environment. Perhaps the Minister of Finance came closest to suggesting a solution when he challenged us all to help produce a pragmatic set of Canadian approaches which would be based on our own experiences and institutions and which would avoid doctrinaire principles that might prove extremely difficult to discard.

Contributors

CLAUDE BISSELL, President, University of Toronto

V. W. BLADEN, Professor, Department of Political Economy, University of Toronto

F. C. BURNET, Employee Relations Manager, Canadian Industries Limited

JOHN J. DEUTSCH, Professor, Department of Economics, Queen's University

WILLIAM DODGE, Executive Vice-President, Canadian Labour Congress

M. W. FARRELL, Economist, The Steel Company of Canada Limited

JOHN L. FRYER, Director of Research, Canadian Labour Congress

ARTHUR KRUGER, Professor, Department of Political Economy, University of Toronto

H. I. MACDONALD, Chief Economist, Government of Ontario

D. L. MCQUEEN, Economic Council of Canada

E. P. NEUFELD, Professor, Department of Political Economy, University of Toronto

GRANT L. REUBER, Department of Economics, University of Western Ontario

FORREST L. ROGERS, Economic Adviser, The Bank of Nova Scotia

ARTHUR M. ROSS, Commissioner, United States Bureau of Labor Statistics

ROBERT SAUVÉ, General Secretary, Confederation of National Trade Unions

HON. MITCHELL SHARP, Minister of Finance, Government of Canada

ARTHUR J. SMITH, Economic Council of Canada

DAVID C. SMITH, Professor, Department of Economics, Queen's University

W. DONALD WOOD, Director, Industrial Relations Centre, Queen's University

CANADIAN UNIVERSITY PAPERBOOKS

Related titles in the series